Gestalt Therapy and Spiritual Perspectives:
The InnerSense Collection

Gestalt Therapy and Spiritual Perspectives:
The InnerSense Collection

Edited by Brian O'Neill

Ravenwood Press

Developed and Published by the
Ravenwood Press a subsidiary of the
Illawarra Gestalt Centre.
Po Box 141 Peregian Beach
Queensland 4573
AUSTRALIA.

Cover illustration, text design and art work: B O'Neill
Made and printed in Australia by University of Wollongong Printery

ISBN applied for. 9781482572711

For more information on Ravenwood Press
Email: boneill@uow.edu.au
Website: www.illawarragestalt.org

 Or write to

Brian O'Neill
Illawarra Gestalt @peregian
Po Box 141 Peregian Beach
Queensland 4573
Australia

I   D e d i c a t i o n   I

To students, faculty and friends of the Illwarra
Gestalt Centre and the New Church in Australia
for their willingness to make the journey
on such a great adventure.

I   Acknowledgements   I

The InnerSense Journal would not exist without the continuing support of so many people including

Seán Gaffney; Anne Maclean; Yaro Starak;
Gary (Jase) Hodson; Martine Negro;Tracy Santos;
Anne Leibig; Kerry Shipman; Julian Duckworth;
Rodney Cole; Renata Drtina; Mala Henderson;
Garry Lake; Laurie Levine; Ben O'Neill; Ian Arnold;
Anne Kelliher; Mark Ryan; Lesley Withey;
Sheryl Wiffen; Esperanza Cardona.

Gestalt Therapy and Spiritual Perspectives:

The InnerSense Collection

Gestalt therapy and spiritual perspectives.

Dying to Live
Tracy Santos 17

On Finding My Way
Seán Gaffney 47

A Transpersonal Search for Meaning
Yaro Starak 59

Gestalt Therapy as a Spiritual Practice
Lesley Withey 67

Kahuna Body Work
Sara Gylany 85

A Journey through Mourning
Seán Gaffney 95

Spirituality and Counselling: Not so Strange 141
Bedfellows *Anne Kelliher*

Inviting the Angel: Counselling and Therapy 183
as Sacred Work *Mark Ryan*

Intimacy and Couples Therapy
Esperanza Cardona 195

Observing Grief
Gary Hodson   203

J stands for Resilience
Sheryl Wiffen   215

Still...On My Way
Seán Gaffney PhD   223

The Whole of Life — a Gestalt
Anne Maclean   245

Climbing Through the Scaffolding of Beliefs ~
A Reflection   *Kerry Shipman*   251

Sitting Still in ElderSpirit Community
Anne Leibig   261

My Experience of Touching Death
Jase C. Hodson   265

Introduction

Brian O'Neill

It is clear that as we enter this new millennium there is an awakening happening in the wider society. Many people complain about the rate of change in the world today. The development of technologies, particularly the computer technologies, has lead to a bigger, faster, more globally connected world. We of the Westernised world are at different poles to those who exist in less economically fortunate countries.

Yet as we gain in wealth and technology, we seem to lose in social disruption. Drug abuse and crime are not decreasing. Violence seems to be escalating. Since the end of World War II there have only been two days when the world was at peace - the two days immediately following the war's end.

Less and less people are attending a religious organisation while most indicate they believe in the spiritual. We do not seem to have gone anywhere fast in answering the questions of "who are we" and "why are we here". Our progress seems only matched by our devolution into a chaotic life of modern living.

It is at such times that it is recognised by the ancient wisdoms that transitions are at hand. Like the movement from sleeping to waking, we are on the threshold of new ways of being in the world. The "60s was one attempt at this with the hippy culture and peace movements - *all you need is love.*" Yet in such times we witnessed assassinations of people that the world viewed champions of justice and freedom, such as Martin Luther King and JFK.

In an abreaction to events in the USA and Vietnam our Western world retreated to the frivolity of the '70s and the selfish commercialism of the '80s. The '90s saw another transition to economic rationalism. The new millennium and the year 2001 was memorable world-wide with the impact of tensions erupting into the aftermath of the September 11th bombing in the USA.

It is at such times of change and turmoil that it becomes clear there is a social awakening in progress. All ancient religious texts, and particularly the Old and New Testaments show these repetitive patterns of the destruction of the old as the new emerges.

I believe we are awakening to the spiritual ground of our being. We are beginning to realise the emptiness of pursuing that which the Buddha states is liable to decay and death (the Ignoble Quest) and are beginning the Noble Quest - to search for that which is undying and immortal.

With the work of Carl Jung and others, people are becoming aware who we experience as our "self" during the day is not the whole story. In some ways we could say we are an illusion, but an illusion or appearance which is as real as the tiger which chased the Wise Man up the tree. He had just said to the king "all the world is an illusion" just before the tiger appeared, "so why are you up the tree?" queried the king. "Ah," he said, "because some illusions as more real than other!"

Part of this illusion or appearance is that we are separate compartments of self - Body, Mind and Soul. In our present conscious existence of the normal waking world we are aware of aspects of our being which include that which we can say is in this physical plane called Body, that which we experience as connected to an "inner" reality which we call Mind, and that which is bigger than us, yet essentially our essence, that we call Soul.

~~~~~~~

This book is a collection of gestalt therapy writers and counsellors who have an interest in these wider realities which may be called spiritual. They come from across Australia and around the world - from Sweden, USA, England, Ireland and New Zealand. They all are familiar with what the gestalt therapist Wilson van Dusen termed *"The Country of Spirit"*. They have each contributed to *InnerSense: A Journal of Spiritual Life* and their writing is collected here in one volume for gestalt therapists (and interested others).

They each provide their flavor and viewpoint of how gestalt therapy intersects with the rest of life. Each tells a story of what is important to them - some in an academic fashion, some as an expression of how they integrate gestalt therapy with their work and life, and others who deeply enter into their most challenging experiences and share them with us in such an open and inspiring way. Each is unique. Each is a great read. Together the offer much that is a rich interface between gestalt therapy, spirituality and life.

On their behalf, I welcome you to their Country of Spirit.

Dying to Live

by

Tracy Santos

There are moments, occasional and intense, when I experience my mortality like a thorn on a glorious rose. I lose sight of the flower and am left hanging on the edge of the thorn. It is uncomfortable and there is a big drop below me. I look down, and don't even recognize the landscape. The unknown-ness is deafening. As my fear grows, the distance of the fall and the impending danger becomes greater. My anxiety and sense of peril escalates.

In these moments I become entirely focused on the limitation of my physical body. I remember that one day, in some way, I will die, and its likely there will be pain involved. I feel deeply baffled by how "I" could possibly end, with no assurance of what happens next. Then, the traffic light turns green and my attention turns to pressing the accelerator, and which street I need to turn into next. I am rescued, temporarily, from my precarious position on the thorn; or, so it seems.

The reality however, is that I was not rescued from this predicament; it was only my awareness of this truth that retreated. The knowledge of my mortality and the accompanying anxiety still live inside me, simmering, and no doubt manifesting in all sorts of neurotic ways. Laura Perls, a renowned Gestalt psychotherapist had strong feelings about this subject;

"I am deeply convinced the basic problem, not only of therapy, but of life, is how to make life livable for a being whose dominant characteristic is his awareness of himself as a unique individual, on the one-hand, and of his mortality on the other hand. The first feeling, that is, feeling we are individuals that are unique, gives us a sense of overwhelming importance. The other feeling, that we will die, gives us a feeling of fear and frustration. Suspended between these two poles, he vibrates in a state of inevitable tension and anxiety that, at least to modern western man, seems un-relievable. This causes neurotic solutions that are prevalent not only in our patients, but to greater or lesser extent in our total culture" (Perls in Fagan and Shepherd, 1970 ,128)

How can we find an understanding of ourselves that will allow alleviation of this tension and... an emergence of greater wisdom in our own lives and our communities? Surely, it is no coincidence that all the great spiritual paths of humankind include meditations on death as an essential lane on the road towards inner peace and awakening.

The indication is that deep in the human soul there is wisdom that knows that reflection and meditation on death is imperative in order to open to the wholeness of living, and the wholeness of our 'self'. Yet our culture actively avoids such contemplation.

Almost nine years ago I gave birth to my first child, a beautiful baby girl named Tasha, who unexpectedly died after five days outside my womb. In five days I experienced birth, initiation into motherhood and the profound joy of life beginning, and then, five days later, the death of this little darling that had only just entered our world. I journeyed from elation and fulfillment, to disbelief and excruciating emotional pain. It was Tasha's death that inspired and compelled me to figure out how could I live, and thrive, in the world without her, and with the pain and bewilderment that arose from being left behind when she went away. It was her death that propelled me on this journey into examining the relationship between death and life and love, and it is with her inspiration that I continue this exploration.

The significance of 'being with' our mortality, really holding it and looking at it directly in the eyes, is not just so we might be prepared when the time comes to die. All the literature, all the talks with friends who have had proximity to death, and from my own experience, all the evidence indicates that accepting and knowing our mortality, openly and willingly, is that which allows the possibility of living fully as a aware, authentic and loving human being.

> Our culture is in a remarkable period of decadence, which means cultural death and the evaporation of values – loss of soul. The best remedy for disease always mirrors the ailment. In a period of waning we need instructions on how to die with grace and beauty. If we learn how to care for each other in our dying, we may discover how to be with each other in our living. (Thomas Moore in Murphy, 1999: p. xiii)

My sincere interest is to explore the richness that can emerge in a life (and a world) when mortality is accepted rather than denied, and perceiving the beauty of the rose includes the virtues of the thorn.

Denying death

> To be whole we must deny nothing. (Levine, 1982 p. 11)

After Tasha died, I had to face the inevitable meeting of others reactions to her death. There were a couple of friends who just didn't mention it at all when I saw them. For me this was bizarre and kind of offensive, but these people were later able to explain that they just couldn't face the fact of 'it' so they ignored the truth of 'it'. Here seemed to be another example of the pathology in our 'modern' culture to believe that if we ignore our mortality and/or attempt to defy the evidence of it, that we recognize as our physical body deteriorates, we will be protected from death. The dominant values of our culture have become appearances and accumulation of as much material wealth, power and status as possible. The consequence, as Thomas Moore says, is a loss of soul.

In the quotation stated previously, Laura Perls talked about the polarity that exists within us, between a sense of our overwhelming importance, and the fear and frustration generated by contemplations of mortality. The image I hold in my mind is of our society clinging to the pole which represents their importance, sense of uniqueness and control; while deliberately ignoring the pole which symbolizes our fragile physical existence. People are desperately beautifying this 'pole'; building new supports for this pole, but... inevitably the pole will not be able to withstand the pressure. The pole was not intended to be a solitary source of support, and the hangers on don't belong there. Like a confused fish jumping into a boat thinking it might buy more life, it may thrash around for a while on the deck, and though the thrashing looks vital and dynamic, it really is an indication of intense imbalance and distress. The fish's approach is misguided and a bit stupid. Similarly, we seem to be doing a bit too much thrashing about, with personal and professional goals which do not serve us in living a deeply satisfying life or preparing to live, and die, with grace and acceptance.

The efforts to avoid aging and death in our advanced society are constant. Medical technology, plastic surgery and genetic research are all dedicated to prolonging, beautifying or replicating life. (Murphy, 1999: p. 46)

Death, and life threatening illness are considered the enemy to be fought at all costs, especially by health care professionals. It is as though longevity is considered the goal of life, but "is longevity all we aspire to?" (Lambert, 1996:3) For me, losing a baby was a profound opportunity to reflect on what makes a life valuable or worthwhile. Was Tasha's life less meaningful or worthwhile than my own, or my ninety year old neighbours', because it was relatively brief? I don't believe so, more so, it is our limited perception of human life, or life in general, which narrows our perceptions of meaning or worth.

Still, there exists a tendency to cling to these technologies or ideals as though they were gods, giving them power over our bodies, our idea of ourselves and our sense of hope. In lieu of an alternate value or belief system, it is in technology and materialism that so many find meaning and purpose in life.

I believe that people are struggling to meet their need for meaning and fulfillment because they have lost touch with what their needs are and who is the self who has needs. We persist with our desperate attempts to control our mortality; the ever increasing rates of depression, feelings of alienation, suicide, and drug dependence are some blatant indicators that our culture is descending into a swamp of soulless values and suffocating personal ethics.

In 1973 Earnest Becker published his Pulitzer Prize-winning *Denial of Death.* In this book Becker also expounded the existential position that the qualities of being human include some that we embrace and others that repulse and terrify us. He theorized that culture and personality develops to help us see the world in such a way that the anxiety caused by the awareness of death is muted or staved off until death is imminent. He even goes so far as to say that;

> And I think, from my point of view, a large part
> of what we call character, the human character,
> the mechanisms of defense, and so on, are really
> a style that we build to deny our own mortality.
> To deny the fact that we are so fragile. So that as
> you grow up, you can feel pretty much confident
> that you control your own life and death. The

sign that you are a mature person is your belief that you control your own life and death, if you work at it correctly. You wash your hands to avoid germs, you drive carefully, you perform in the corporation, you put a certain amount of money into the bank, you try to get good seats on the airplane, and you're juggling constantly. In the background, of course, is the fear that you don't. (Becker, 1993 p. 9)

Woody Allen demonstrated this approach succinctly and very amusingly when he said "Everyone dies, I am hoping in my case they will make an exception". (Allen in Lampert, 1996 p. 1) Every time I read the quote I smile wondering just who he thinks 'they' are.

In this context, all these soulless attempts at feeling important and in control, suddenly appear as transparent attempts to avoid contemplating and accepting the mystery of our existence, and the impermanence of our human life, exposing the fact that we generally have inadequate personal and cultural resources to reconcile these tensions.

To embrace or eclipse mystery?

I am drawn to the term Mystery as a reference to encompass that which we do not know and that which we do not understand. This word generates a lot of energy for me and I feel a fresh sense of excitement each time use it and consider its expansive meaning.

Earnest Becker (1973) tells about having been asked to give input to a local nursery co-op discussion as to whether it was the appropriate time to tell the children where they come from i.e. the sperm and the egg.

> So I said, "Well, if you want to lie to them". Everybody in the room turned and looked at me. They said, "What do you mean lie to them?" I said. "Well, you don't know where they came from, do you? Sperm and the egg is only one step in the causal chain that remains fundamentally a mystery, right? You don't really know where children come from." They didn't like that. They really didn't like that. They thought it was dishonest to tell them it was a mystery. And yet, you know, the one thing we are learning about children is that when they

ask you questions like that, they really want to know what they are doing here. Children ask religious questions that we repress. And we refuse to give them religious answers which are really the only ones that mean anything. Naturalistic answers don't answer questions. So they're asking us "Who am I?" The kid wants to know who he is and what he is doing on this planet. And we don't know, so we lie to him and tell him how he came to be here, which is not really how he came to be, since we don't know. And the one dangerous thing we do with that, however well intentioned we are when we do it, is we *eclipse the dimension of mystery.*

Reading this passage had a significant impact on me and my consideration of the ways in which I, and people generally eclipse the mystery from our world by trying to attach ourselves to things, ideas and people which allow us to feel like we know what it's all about. (Krishnamurti, 1978) People rigidly hold belief systems (in the form of ideas, theories or religions) which provide stories to contextualize our life on the planet, and without wanting to discredit the plethora of beliefs people hold, I do suggest that these systems can have the function or consequence of eclipsing mystery. Such rigidity of idea or belief also could be seen to serve to distract us, or help us avoid the greatest mystery: death and the void.

In the space beyond our sense of uniqueness and self importance lies mystery. Perhaps it is also the tendency to eclipse mystery that greatly exacerbates the tension between the poles Laura Perls talked about, and contributes to the neurotic symptoms of our selves and society. So how to embrace mystery? Wilson Van Dusen (1992 p, 6) gives an insight into how we might; "I am mystery, looking at mystery, appreciating mystery. The very essence of the mystical experience is to appreciate this – what is....There is a tremendous now-ness to the mystical experience. It is as though all that ever was passes through this present into all there will ever be. One rests in such a moment. Questions have no place. Doubts are absent. Here, thus, it is."

By embracing mystery we loosen the hold on what we need to know, what we need to prove and what we need to be. By being with 'what is', rather than trying to control ourselves and our environment, we can safely start to edge away from the beautified pole which symbolizes our attachment to our uniqueness, and have a little swim in the sea of mystery. With this new buoyancy we are able to entertain a whole new range of human emotion and experience.

Being with 'what is' and accepting.

> And the questioning springs from what is most vulnerable, unformulable, within us. It accepts inherent contradictions: failure with success, weakness with strength, death with life. And it returns to the Tao, but not comfortably. We go with this flow only at a cost, for it asks of us a yielding in which nothing is fixed, in which we become, like it, a mystery.
>
> But in the end there is no other way to see things plain or, without any pressure or constraint, to know ourselves. When we let things be as they are, we shall have become as we are. (Lao-Tzu in Schoen, 1994)

This emphasis on learning to be present with *what is*, is one of the central tenants of many spiritual texts and practices, including Taoism and Buddhist traditions. From my understanding and personal experience, having been involved with Buddhist orientated meditation practices and teachings for many years, the state of being with and appreciating 'what is' involves a state of detachment from wanting things to be or not to be a certain way. This implies a deep state of acceptance towards life and all it offers us as experiences, including death.

The pain I experienced after Tasha died was intense and consuming, as was the confusion and bewilderment. One day I was a new mother to my beautiful baby, the next I was without my child, milk leaking from my breasts, my whole being yearning for her. But she was gone. Nothing I could say or do would change this. No explanations or theories about why she died could change what had happened; I realized it was all a mystery. I began to realize that the only way for me to continue to feel as though I were living well in myself and in the world was to not think something wrong had happened, or something bad, but rather to learn how to just be with the truth of it. Tasha died. She's gone. And though I feel the tears welling while typing these words, and I miss her every day, and part of me will always wish she was here with me; I also hold within myself a calm place of acceptance of what happened and what is happening; even an appreciation.

Perhaps instead of fighting to feel meaningful and worthwhile (or fighting to not feel fear or anxiety), if we stop, and be as we are, we might find a meaning in our lives (and death) we never knew.

Impermanence and who we are.

In Buddhist writings, the foundation for the emphasis on being with 'what is', and 'who we are' in the moment is connected to the *idea* of impermanence. I used the word *idea*, because I felt hesitation in using the word truth, yet in my experience and opinion 'impermanence' is one of the only truths we have as human beings. Everything, including myself, is constantly in flux. And though the world may be superficially perceived as solidity, this is illusion. In The Art of Living by William Hart (1987), a Vipassana meditation student of S.N. Goenka, he dissects the physiological reality of our physical form:

Let us begin with the physical aspect. This is the most obvious, the most apparent portion of ourselves, readily perceived by all the senses.

And yet how little we really know about it. Superficially one can control the body; it moves and acts according to conscious will. But on another level, all the internal organs function beyond our control, without our knowledge. At a subtler level we know nothing, experientially, of the incessant biochemical reactions occurring within each cell of the body. But this is still not the ultimate reality of the material phenomenon. Ultimately the seemingly solid body is composed of subatomic particles and empty space. What is more, even these subatomic particles have no real solidity; the existence span of one of them is less than a trillionth of a second. Particles continuously arise and vanish, passing into and out of existence, like a flow of vibrations. This is the ultimate reality of the body, of all matter, discovered by the Buddha 2500 years ago. (Hart, 1987 p. 25)

In 1991 I attended my first ten day Vipassana meditation retreat in the Blue Mountains outside of Sydney. We were instructed to sit and observe our body, mind and breath (with observation and awareness, rather than response), for eleven hours a day. It was on the fourth day that I had an experience that changed my life. Paradoxically, as Arnold Beisser suggested, this change occurred when I experienced myself as I was, although it appeared that I was doing nothing.

On this day, for several consecutive moments, I observed with great clarity, the dance of impermanence within my being. I felt the arising and passing away of energy in my body. I felt the space that exists between the particles that blurs the boundary between myself and the person beside me and all else. I experienced a connectedness to others and to life that I had never felt in such a concentrated way before. I experienced a stream of awareness that felt simultaneously pure in each moment, and, timeless. It was as though by experiencing the truth of impermanence with awareness and acceptance, I arrived fully within myself, and by wholly embracing life in the moment I experienced a state of calm which felt deathless.

> What a beautiful and what a healing mystery it is that from contemplating, continually and fearlessly, the truth of change and impermanence, we come slowly to find ourselves face to face, in gratitude and joy, with the truth

of the changeless, with the truth of the deathless, unending nature of mind. (Rinpoche, 1992 p. 40)

Was this what John Paul Satre was speaking of when he said 'It is in Nothingness alone that Being can be surpassed'? (Satre, 1943 p. 51) I am not sure, but I do know that after that meditation I experienced a kind of stripping away of parts of my ego. After this experience I could no longer easily hold certain ideas of myself as fixed or rigid, my sense of my place in the world became more fluid. The things that I met in the calm, beyond the flux, were *love, awareness and acceptance*. And in facing Tasha's death, and my own, these three things have become my greatest resource for living and facing my own mortality.

In the Tibetan Book of Living and Dying, Sogyal Rinpoche says that 'one of the chief reasons we have so much anguish and difficulty facing death is that we ignore the truth of impermanence'(1992 p. 25) Alongside this is the suggestion that meditations on death are the best strategy for integrating the truth of our impermanence:

Of all footprints

That of the elephant is supreme:

Of all mindfulness mediations

That on death is supreme

> (The Buddha, in Rinpoche, 1992 p. 26)

If we have an understanding that everything is constantly changing and that this is, paradoxically, perhaps the only thing there is to hold onto, our only lasting possession, then we then will be able to hold a deep understanding as to why the only thing we really have is *now*.

How could all this serve to alleviate the existential angst or the unrelievable tension Laura Perls spoke of? Well, perhaps we can find a place where we can embrace mystery and learn to be with 'what is' and 'who we are' in each moment, while understanding that an acceptance of impermanence doesn't undermine what we do and who we are. On the contrary, it gives us a new sense of who we are and our potential. It gives us the opportunity to discover who we are in the light of our impermanence, *and* beyond the flux of things, people, ideas and physical states.

The self in life.

"What is the self"? The trend we say developing in the skin self and the social self continues at the theological level. We saw that the self is dependent on the environment and lives in a network of relationships. The idea that the self is totally separate is fundamentally an illusion and is actually a very poor way of conceiving humanness. (Van Dusen, 1992 p. 45)

The issue is where one will pin one's personal identity. One fundamental answer that emerges from the study of many myths, religions, and one's own experience is: let the personal identity be everything and nothing simultaneously. When one carefully explores the boundaries of personal identity, they expand beyond all expectations. The broadening of the boundaries may well be the root of wisdom. (Van Dusen 1992 p. 33)

And what is a life? Michael Holmes (1998), who has supported many people in their dying process, shares his pragmatic perspective on life and death. He explains that, 'maintaining a physical body requires an enormous degree of focused energy which can only be kept up for a certain period of time...being physical at all is miraculous, but that sooner or later this concentration of energy will fade away' (Holmes 1998 p. 20).

Here, the self is simply and calmly perceived as organically emerging, and then, quite naturally, fading back. There is an ease and acceptance in his words. When I read his words for the first time, I experienced a clarity about my life emerging temporarily (being minutes or decades), and then fading again in order that a new life may emerge. As Howard Adams in The Search for Wholeness (1993 p. 87) says; 'Death is essentially returning to renew your contact with your potential'.

Whether this potential involves returning to another body or to another state of being is another conversation for another time. Differing opinions about life after death does not alter the reality that we will die to this physical body.
So.....

With all our modern advancements we seem to be losing touch with our 'selves' and our souls. Death is ritually alienated, rather than incorporated, into our culture. This rejection of our essential nature leaves us with a poverty, disguised by our wealth. We are taught to avoid pain and perceive illness, and the prospect of death, as the enemy. Yet, Elizabeth Kubler-Ross(1970), who's' life's work was dedicated to her dying patients, believed that *'in every suffering there is a seed for growth, an opportunity offered to evolve and that is the only purpose for our being here on earth'*.

I wonder if constant attempts to reject suffering, of ourselves and others, and denying its value, exaggerates our suffering. Maybe if we move into acceptance, observation and love, then our actions will be born from this womb, and suffering may bring opportunities for our hearts to open and our spirit to awaken.

I-thou, love and death and the end.....

The boundaries of my body blur, I am, after all a collection of vibrations, traveling through time and space. Superficially I exist as separate, but I also exist as interconnected and interdependent with other beings and all that exists in my environment. As I will die, so to will all that lives around me, my parents, my children, the trees, the animals, the planet. A great virtue in meditating on our own mortality is the consequence that we will be better prepared to support and care for others when they face these anxieties and when they approach the time of death.

> Once you have faced your own finiteness and accepted it, you will see that life becomes much more meaningful and more valuable. These people who have truly faced their own finiteness will be much better equipped to help dying patients. (Kubler-Ross, 1970 p. 21)

My heart is whispering to me in its tender, but clear voice. It is reminding me of the glorious rose and its soft pink petals. It is reminding me of love. For what use are theories and ideas if they are lived only in the mind?

> Yes, in essence I and Thou is simple. Thou is the other, met openly and without design. Love is caring for thou, and it tempers self-assertion. Without love, the other becomes an It, any use of whom is, in a sense, a misuse. (Buber, 1970)

I will conclude by sharing the story of Tashas' death and what she taught me about dying and living:

In the last hours of Tashas' life, when we knew she only had a short time to live, my husband and I lay with her between us on a bed, in a small room in the hospital, and tried to face her death and our lives. These were probably the most devastating, confusing, painful and bountiful eight hours of my life to date. The thought of my little girl being in pain was excruciating. Knowing all the systems of her body were failing. My own feelings of pain and emotional distress were excruciating. I felt a strong desire for her to die, for her pain to be over, for the agonizing suspense I was experiencing to come to an end. I felt the urge to avoid suffering, my own and hers. I felt resistance.

The doctor's had suggested she would live two hours once coming off the life support, and seven hours later we were still there with her. One of the nurses came in to tell me my father was on the phone and I decided to take the call. I told Dad of my desire for her to go, and he said to me calmly "Trace, just love her, every moment you can". It was as though God was talking through my father. I hold a deep sense of gratitude, to my father *and* life, for these words at this time.

I walked back into the room and embraced Tasha in my arms, while laying against Luis on the bed. I allowed the fear, the anxiety and the 'wanting it to be another way' to fade. I allowed my being to fill with love and acceptance. It felt profoundly beautiful, it felt healing. Soon after this she died.

In those hours before my Dad called I experienced within myself the distraction away from love that comes from wanting things to be other than they are. Tasha inspired me to live, and die, with acceptance and grace.

The tendency is for the word dying to be associated with the point at which a fatal prognosis is given, and yet in a sense, we are all dying from birth. Not only that, but we could die unexpectedly at any moment. The reality of our mortality is unavoidable, and life *is* a dying process.

Though my tendency is to consider this perspective morbid, this is largely due a persistent loyalty I have to the pervasive denial of death, and the idea of myself as fixed and separate. A loyalty not supported by my experience.

It is the stripping back of false loyalties and identifications, and the uncovering of an authentic awareness which allows us to discover who we really are, and renders us the opportunity to learn how to 'be with' who we discover ourselves to be.

We walk a precarious path through life, the destination is unknown, the scenery is sometimes grotesque and scary, sometimes stunningly beautiful, but with the companionship of awareness, acceptance and love, we can walk with eyes open, willingly, into the unknown. Living well and dying well become synonymous. Living and dying merge into wholeness.

References

Adams, H. (1993) The Search for Wholeness. Gestalt Institute of Australia. Springwood.

Becker, E. (1993) Growing Up Rugged: Fritz Perls and Gestalt Therapy. The Gestalt Journal Vol 14, 2

Becker, E. (1973) The Denial of Death. Free Press. New York. USA

Buber, M. (1970) I and Thou. Scribner's Sons. New York. USA

Fagan, J., & Shepherd, I, L. (eds) (1970) Gestalt Therapy Now. Science and Behaviour Books, Inc. USA

Feinstein, D., & Elliot Mayo, P. (1990) Rituals for Living and Dying: How We Can Turn Loss and The Fear of Death into an Affirmation of Life. Harper Collins. NY. USA

Hart, W. (1987) The Art of Living. Harper and Row. USA

Holmes, M., (1998) Crossing the Creek (www. crossingthecreek.com)

Krishnamurti. J. (1978) The Wholeness of Life. Krishnamurti Foundation India. Madras. India

Kubler-Ross, E. (1973) On Death and Dying. Fletcher and Son Ltd.. Norwich. Great Britian

Kubler-Ross, E. (1974) Questions and Answers on Death and Dying. Macmillion Publishing Co. NY. USA

Lampert, R. (1996) The Case for Going Gentle. www.gestalt.org/gentle.htm

Levine, S. (1982) Who Dies? An Investigation of Conscious Living and Conscious Dying. Anchor Books. USA

Murphy, M. (MD) (1999) The Wisdom of Dying: Practices for Living. Element Books. Boston. USA

Rinpoche, S. (1992) The Tibetan Book of Living and Dying. Rider. London. GB

Rutledge, T. (2002) Embracing Fear. Harper. San Fran. USA

Satre, J-P. (1956) Being and Nothingness. Washington Square Press. NY. USA

Schoen, S. (PhD) (1994) Presence of Mind: Literary and Philosophical Roots of a Wise Psychotherapy. The Gestalt Journal Press. NY. USA

Zen Master Wu Kwang (Shrobe, R.) (2004) An Exploration of the Zen Kong-An and Gestalt Impasse. Kwan Um School of Zen. (www.kwanumzen.com)

On Finding My Way

by

Seán Gaffney

A month before my eighteenth birthday, I entered Mount Saint Joseph Cistercian monastery, Roscrea, Ireland, as a novice monk (= future priest). My path there had been uncharacteristically crooked. All of my dear mother's middle-class snobbery had (damn – HAS) been passed on to me, so I always go for the top wherever I am...

Here, however, I had succeeded in getting names and addresses mixed up. Mount Melleray is/was the name of the main Cistercian monastery in Ireland, the oldest, the mother-house, so clearly "the original and best". Mount Melleray is in County Cork. I had sent my letter of interest in exploring a possible monastic vocation to Mount Melleray (right name), Roscrea (wrong place), County Tipperary (and wrong again!)...and it had been delivered to the Novice Master at Mount Saint Joseph, Roscrea. Father Ambrose, as he was named, had replied warmly and invited me to Roscrea for an

47

interview. So a year before my entrance, I had made my way to the second best of the two Cistercian monasteries then in Ireland, hoping to make the best of a bad mistake.

And so I found myself accepted and entering...exchanging my clothes for medieval long-johns, white woollen socks, and a plain white soutane-like habit. All my hair was shaved off.

Thus began a core experience in my life, a defining experience, a resounding "failure" which transformed and is still transforming my life. In fact, defining my life. And you, dear reader, are participating in this as you read...

I immersed myself fully in monastic life. Father Ambrose later told me that I had taken to it like a duck to water, and he had envied me the ease with which I embraced what had been for him a distressful period of doubt and discomfort. Apparently, my confessor, Father Thomas, had also indicated that all was well with me.

And then I ran straight into a wall, stopped dead in my tracks. I was moved to the Infirmary for a period of rest, with relaxed rules. The Assistant Novice Master, Father Canice, visited me and told me of his decision to leave the Cistercian Order and join the Capuchin Friars, a reformed branch of the Franciscans. Interestingly, the

Capuchins had been my first choice when I first began considering the priesthood, an interest which had shifted towards the full monastic life of enclosed silence as it was practiced then by the Order of Cistercians of the Strict Observance, their full title. After Father Canice's visit, I felt strengthened in my choice and my resolve.

Then came the first of many visits and conversations with Father Ambrose. He had reached a decision about me which he had thought deeply and prayed about as well as talking it through with Father Canice, my confessor Father Thomas, The Prior, Father Lawrence and The Abbot, Dom Camillus. His decision was that I should leave. His feeling was that I was wasted in a monastery. He saw me as a preacher, a teacher, someone who communicated his world to others. An enclosed monastic life of prayer and silence was stifling who I was, not developing me. God, he said, would not call me to a life which lessened who I was.

I argued, fought with every fibre and nerve in me, held out, held on, pushed, asked to talk with the others involved and named...and always came back to hearing the calm statement that I was a preacher, a teacher of others, a communicator whose vocation was not yet clear – except that it was not as a Cistercian monk.

Finally, I left the monastery, filled with my sense of failure. I had failed to become a monk. I had even failed to complete my novitiate period of two full years.

All the fanfare of my leaving family and friends was now replaced by the embarrassed silence of a low-key return. Over a period of two years, I made efforts to re-join, always with the same consequence: this was not my vocation, I needed to let go and find it, maybe still the priesthood though not necessarily so. Just let go, follow your path as it comes, pray, trust, be open...

My final attempt was at the new foundation by the Cistercians of Roscrea, at Mount Bolton, Athy, County Carlow, where Father Ambrose was now Dom Ambrose, Abbot of the new community. He actually greeted me on my first visit there with a huge smile, a warm welcome, and a loud, laughing "NO!". So I finally gave up.

Having had a number of temporary jobs – night worker at the Irish Post, goods clerk with the Irish Railways, builders' labourer – I now moved to England to become a Student Psychiatric Nurse. By the end of my first year there, I had been chosen to join a specialist programme for a combination Registered Psychiatric and General Nurse qualification. I was well on my way into a career in nursing, with a choice of future paths.

Then a female patient claimed that she had been raped by a male nurse. Her only description was "an Irish junior"- our uniforms defined us as Staff, Senior (qualified) or Junior (student). So the Hospital Board, faced with a police inquiry and a major scandal if the supposed incident were investigated – whatever the outcome – decided in its infinite British wisdom to fire ALL Irish student nurses, more than half of the student body at the time. Thus ended my career in nursing...though my training stayed with me!

I moved to London, and straight into the 1960s.
If it could be done, I did it.
If it could be tested, I tested it.

I needed jobs to pay my rent and buy my food and the like. Careers were something the others had, not us, certainly not me. Free and in free-fall, I had a ball...endlessly!

Then my alcoholic father was imprisoned for bad debts, and I hastily returned to Dublin. Amongst my many short-term jobs was a period as Front of House manager for a travelling repertory company. It was during this period that I met my Swedish future wife.

So I returned to England, she and I moved in together and eventually married. I needed a job...and got one with an Italian domestic appliance company. Within a year, I had moved up in the ranks into middle management – and a position as trainer for new staff. Later, I moved company, and found myself as Senior Sales Trainer and Customer Relations Trainer. And so began a period as Management Trainer, first in England, then Ireland, then Sweden.

We had moved to Sweden in 1975. My early jobs were partly as an independent Management Trainer in English for multinational Swedish companies, and also as an adult education teacher. I took a post graduate qualification in the Teaching of English as a Foreign Language (TOEFL) and eventually got a position as an English Teacher at the Stockholm School of Economics (SSE). Within a few years, I was head of the Languages and Communication Department at the School as well as a lecturer at the Institute of International Business at SSE in Cross-cultural Management. This was soon followed by a senior Lecturer position at the SDA Business School of Universitá Bocconi, Milan, Italy as well as The Riga School of Economics, Latvia.

While all of these things were happening I started on and completed my Diploma in Gestalt Therapy, my

Diploma in Gestalt Organizational & Systems Dynamics and started my Ph.D in Gestalt with Groups.

And then I found myself in Ireland in the late summer of 2000 as faculty for one of the Gestalt programmes with which I work. I had hired a car and was driving to the far south-west from Dublin Airport. The road passes by Roscrea. I found myself stopping there to get a mobile-phone battery charger...and looking at the road-sign to Mount Saint Joseph Monastery. And deciding that I was too busy and did not have the time. So I drove on.

Our usual end of session faculty meetings were over quickly. Colleagues were leaving for the States. I found myself with a day to spare in terms of my planned travel back to Sweden, where I still live.

So I started out on my journey back to Dublin Airport. After a few hours, I was approaching Roscrea again, this time from the opposite direction. I knew that I could have driven directly to the Guest House at the monastery, yet chose not to. I tried a couple of roadside hotels around Roscrea, without any luck – there was a big local sports event on and everywhere was full. I drove on, intending now to go straight back to Dublin. A good hour past Roscrea I saw a sign for a hotel, and drove in. They had a vacancy.

The next morning, I returned to Roscrea and to Mount Saint Joseph. As I arrived, I realized that it was exactly 40 years that week since my formal induction as a novice. I cried. I entered the church. I watched as 12 monks and 1 white-clad novice filed in for midday prayers. Those 40 years earlier, there had been 120 monks and 7 novices. I recognized most of the monks. Their singing was as ragged as I remembered it from my time there, though now weaker. There I sat and listened, tears streaming down my face – as they are now, with the memory of that moment, and a CD of the Monks of Roscrea playing which I got last Christmas from one of my sisters.. I sat still in my place long after the monks had left.

I had not recognized any of my novice friends, and certainly not Father Ambrose. What had happened to them? Like me, out in the world outside our chosen place? And Ambrose dead and buried by now?

I got up to leave, reluctant to take what would probably be my final step out of that world of such deep importance to who I am. Slowly, I began leaving. In the vestibule to the church, there were the usual pamphlets and prayer-sheets. And – could it be true? A photograph of Father Ambrose on a sheet announcing his retirement as Abbot of Mount Bolton – the previous week! Alive and well, and living in Mount Bolton!

Have you ever driven in a car and felt you were flying? Have time and space ever disappeared into abstractions with which you have no time, or space? Has a two-hour journey taken what seems to be five minutes? Has a two-hour journey seemed like a life-time?

I arrived. Well, that is – my body arrived. More than that I cannot say. There was a stillness and restfulness about the place – and then I remembered: yes, our siesta time, from lunch onwards for about 90 minutes.

A relic of our continental roots. So nothing happening here. I went into the church, which was just beginning to be built at my last visit there – the "NO!" visit. Again, I cried, as I am crying now. So much of who I was, became and am is here. Was here at the time I am describing, and is here now as I re-visit it. And not even physically "here" in Mount Bolton, or "here" in Stockholm. No – here in Mount Saint Joseph and my fellow novices, postulants, monks and brothers from that time and place in a world which transcends time and place. Here in a timeless, placeless here and now.

I walked out into the garden. A figure approached me slowly, using two walking-sticks. I knew him well.

Brother Alberic, I thought. We had played with a rugby ball in the corridors of the Guest House before my entry, and later on my return visits when even he shook his head at me to say "no". He looked at me, and greeted me by my monastic name. I did the same with him. He embraced me, and asked "Does Ambrose know that you are here?" I replied that he did not. Brother Alberic transferred a stick to another hand, took my hand in his and said "Brother, you are the last of his novices he knows anything about...he is still in touch with all the rest of you...he will be delighted to meet you."

And so I met Father Ambrose again, after some 35 years. We sat and chatted as if time had both stood still and yet also gone by.

I asked him if he remembered his words to me about teaching, preaching and communicating. "Oh yes" he said, "I do. I have always worried about whether *you* would remember them". So I told him what I now do (see below). We talked about psychotherapy and the confessional, and agreed that the difference is that confession offers that which psychotherapy cannot offer a Catholic, namely forgiveness. We also spoke of a dilemma he had: he had been chosen as the Cistercian

Orders' international advisor on novices. "How could they" he said "of my fifteen novices only two made it through to profession as monks, and only one as a priest". I responded: "Ambrose, that's why. You know who is who. You have helped us who are not ready to find our path in life. You have always supported us to find our vocation."

I spent three hours with Ambrose that afternoon. There is no meeting in my life so far that can match those three hours or their epilogue. None.

Ambrose excused himself to attend Vespers in the church. We agreed to meet and part afterwards. I sat in the church for vespers. Afterwards, I came out and found Ambrose and a vaguely recognisable figure, supported by crutches, waiting by my car. Ambrose said: "you may remember Father Raymond" and gestured towards the figure by my car. Yes – yes, of course I did! Father Raymond!

Father Raymond reached out his hand to shake mine and then said: "Brother, Father Thomas was your confessor. As you know, Thomas was not always in the best of health. So I took over at times as confessor for the novices. I will always remember when you needed a confessor, and were directed to me. I still remember the look of shock on your face at meeting me and not

Thomas. I have always felt that I failed you in some way, and want to tell you how sorry I am. Thomas was a great confessor. I was never as good as he was." After some 40 years, I found myself absolving Father Raymond.

Forgiveness is not to be underestimated.

For the record, I teach in four universities internationally, I teach in eight Gestalt institutes internationally, I supervise Gestalt therapists, I supervise Gestalt OSD consultants, I write on Gestalt in each of the English language journals, I write on MBA teaching, on international consultancy. I communicate my world to others.

And right now, dear reader, I am writing to you on the spirituality of life-coaching by the greatest expert I have ever met – Father Ambrose O.C.S.O – who was in turn supervised by ...well, come on: what/who is your name for Father Ambrose's supervisor?

Whose ultimate client I am...gratefully, and humbly.

A transpersonal search for meaning

by

Yaro Starak

Transpersonal psychology is a school of psychology that studies the transpersonal, the transcendent or spiritual aspects of the human experience. Issues considered in transpersonal psychology include spiritual self-development, peak experiences, mystical experiences, systemic trance and other metaphysical experiences of living.

Transpersonal psychologists see the school as a companion to other schools of psychology that include psychoanalysis, behaviorism, and humanistic psychology. Transpersonal psychology attempts to unify modern psychology theory with frameworks from different forms of mysticism. These vary greatly depending on the origin but include religious conversion, altered states of consciousness, trance and other spiritual practices.

Although Carl Jung and others have explored aspects of the spiritual and transpersonal in their work, transpersonal psychology for the most part has been overlooked by psychologists who are focused on the personal and developmental aspects of the human psyche.

As I began 2008 I thought how much transpersonal psychology has a place in our search for meaning. The New Year has arrived and all the good wishes that were shared over the holidays are now long past. The media continues to expose the horrors and terror that is being inflicted upon humans and nature in many parts of the world accompanied by false ideologies, religious fundamentalism and the struggle for power.

We are entering, more and more, into a vortex of self-destruction based on the illusion and false belief in "our" God. And so the world has changed very little since the evolution of humanity. In psychotherapy we are also entering a place of divisions, a plethora of "treatment" methods for our ills and much confusion about what is good and ethical practice calling for legal management (control) of false practitioners selling solutions to our ills.

For over one hundred years now that we are exploring and researching ways of dealing with the problems of the human psyche and still the outcomes are unclear. However some more recent developments could bring us some hope. Psychology and spirituality seem to be getting closer due to the re-discovery of ancient shamanism and spiritual practices coming from the Eastern traditions that have been little known in the west for thousands of years. Ken Wilber's book on "The Marriage of Sense and Soul" is one example of an attempt at union between science of the West and spirituality of the East.

Nonetheless many people are experiencing a creeping fundamentalism that is creating a new "inquisition" which questions those attempts to 'marry' ancient spiritual practices with hard science. Evangelism in both scientific circles and religious groups are fighting against ways that are touching our most intimate relationships and even re-interpreting the sexual relationships.

This split between sense and soul has created much confusion in people searching for a spiritual understanding and a path of awareness that is one of the most important psycho-spiritual needs today. Many enter this search by way of Yoga (there are many), Tantra, various meditations, the Enneagram and so on. A few join 'growth' weekends with visiting "gurus" and get a sense of temporary well being and talk about their 'virtual transformation' that eventually result in a temporary trance state leading to more confusion later. The most difficult question is still the same: "Who am I?"

There are stories in many journals about the true search of a spiritual Master or Guide that has been able to give the disciple THE WAY. However, where to find such a Master among the thousands of so called 'enlightened' guides that eventually take your money and go home. Many charlatans and New Age marketers can be found on the internet selling everything: from instant 'enlightenment' to Viagra. Zen philosophers for millennia have been saying that if you are confused and do not know what to do, then do no-thing. This will help you to get out of the trance state of the spiritual supermarket and begin a search for a true Master.

The True Master

A spiritual search is not some sort of holidays from reality as it is. It takes more than a week or two of residential seminars where we may feel free to practice our spiritual discipline for a while and then get back to the chores at home. The spiritual path is a constant process of discovery of our own limitations, errors and confusions as we experience life each day.

Most people end up searching for a therapist. A good therapist may be able to help us with ways of achieving a healthier life style or a more satisfactory relationship or a deeper awareness of our blocks to growth or even gain insights how to resolve issues based on a false self. At times a good therapist will be able to guide us to find a spiritual path, but at the end, the full journey is ours alone.

Transpersonal psychology is a branch of psychology that has been attempting to interface between spirituality and modern psychology. Studies conducted to find a definition of a Master have been many and what follows is a summary. The true Master is not a master over others, but a master of himself or herself. The very word and gestures that come from such a master reflect a state of inner wisdom. He has no personal goals, no desire to educate or change but accept things as they are – here and now.

With a true Master we experience our own true Nature and in his silence we find our calm and inner peace. A Master has much to share and not to lead us somewhere. He enables to create a mutual field of energy where disciples can find their own path to selfhood. However, to choose a path to that selfhood with a Master is not easy.

It is a constant challenge; a struggle to transform our old patterns and social conditioning and that process may often be very painful and take a long time. Many choose not to go that way and seek a 'quick fix' instead of developing a long term discipline.

A therapist, no matter how good or capable he or she may be, will never be able to become our spiritual Master. Some therapists may have their own unfinished issues to complete while others will have excellent techniques that will help us to reach a point of resolution of our life issues but at the end, the therapist has to earn a living from the therapy work (called a profession) and therefore very few have been able to dedicate themselves to a spiritual search themselves.

Many people may ask: "Do I really need to have a spiritual master"?...."What for"? Life as it is today has so many distractions that an honest search requires much work and time. A spiritual guide comes when we are ready. This means that we have had a long inner struggle with our self and our shadow. The ancient monks called "the dark night of the soul". Finally such struggle requires help from someone who has been there to guide us into the light.

Yet this struggle is worth-while. Rumi, the great Sufi poet once said: "false gold exists because the real gold exists". The spiritual guide is there to help us to distinguish real gold from false gold. Being clear and authentic in our aim to search for a true spiritual path must begin with the first step and that is meet the guide and then embark on a life-long journey without end.

Today, the word "enlightenment" has been used in so many contexts including in the current New Age marketing of 'spiritual solutions' that is much better to begin with self-understanding and personal growth rather than search for an "enlightenment" formula. In addition, as we grow into more awareness each day, we will be able to assist others in our community to do their personal growth work. As a song states: "we are the world" – the source of all beauty and part of all Nature interconnected with everything that exists.

Most people live in a limited consciousness and therefore inhabit a dark cave (Socrates) and see nothing but their shadows reflected on its walls. They believe that those shadows are THE reality. By opening our eyes and drop the veils of illusion, we may be able to eradicate the evil shadows of cultural conditioning that has been the cause of much pain for millennia.

However, without a spiritual guide who has harnessed the creative energy of passion and therefore of Love for all creation rather than destruction we cannot reach the understanding that brings the peace, harmony and understanding that we are all longing for. Eradicating evil takes a spiritual discipline and not a warrior nature. Allowing the passion without the repression that leads to destruction and imbalance requires understanding and integration of the gift of creative light that comes from the pure centre (heart) of each human being.

Gestalt therapy as a spiritual practice

by

Lesley Withey

This article is an excerpt from my thesis that I completed in becoming accredited as a Gestalt therapist. I asked the question "Can Gestalt be a daily spiritual practice"?

In approaching the topic of Gestalt therapy as a spiritual practice it may be useful to first consider just what is Gestalt and what does a spiritual practice mean to me? How can I live a life that is spiritual in nature and incorporate the principles of Gestalt theory into that?

Gestalt Therapy

To begin with Gestalt therapy, it is seen to have four main aspects which are Phenomenology, Field Theory, Dialogue and Experiment. Let's consider each of these in brief.

Phenomenology, is about the 'here and now', and awareness, the lens through which we look at our experiences to take in this data. In particular it encourages us to be aware of our interpretations as therapists in this process. Yontef (1993) talks about when a phenomenological therapist brackets her own perspective of life and appreciates the equal validity of the client's reality and different set of data, then she can enter the world of her client and not dishonour it.

Dialogue, is how we are together in what Martin Buber has called the 'I/Thou' relationship, and so as I enter the world of my client I must put aside my own phenomenology to understand theirs. Dialogue is lived; it's about being with the 'other' and the contact that happens between us. The relationship grows from the experience of the boundary between 'me' and the 'other'.

Experiment, is the practice of behaviour and 'what and how'. It is what is done in the clinical setting, and not what should or could be. Different techniques are used such as art, guided meditations, bodywork, fantasies, exaggerated body movements etc. Expression of ones feelings using these techniques assist in discovering aspects of self.

These are ways to have contact with our self; a deeper connection and understanding of who we are can give a deeper meaning to our purpose.

Field Theory, This is about who we are in our environment. The centre of Gestalt is Field Theory as shown in the hologram below. Everything is in movement and is affected by everything else. We affect the environment and the environment affects us. Field theory is a way of discovering that can describe the field of which everything is a part. Yontef talks about a Field as being

> "a systematic web of relationships. A totality of mutually influencing forces that together form a unified interactive whole" (Yontef, 1993 p. 295,)

Gestalt was developed over 50 years ago by many influences like Fritz and Laura Perls, and Paul Goodman, and is practised today by therapists all over the world as an evolving and eclectic way of working with clients.

Spirituality and Gestalt therapy

Spirituality for me is about doing and being, i.e. we can 'do' as well as just 'be'. My spirituality from a Gestalt perspective allows me to become centred in the present moment, in the here and now, freed from the confines of the past and the fears of the future. This happens for me not only in my personal life, but also when working in a therapeutic setting.   This belief and philosophy creates harmony for me on a mental, physical, emotional and spiritual level.

Spirituality means many different things to different people and everyone has their own concept of what spirituality is.   Some people when think spirituality is about God and think of what the afterlife will bring for them.   Others may think it's about being 'good' or doing 'good deeds' while here on the earth.

For me, spirituality has become my way of life.   My spirituality is 'now' oriented and this helps me in a therapeutic setting to encourage my clients to be in the 'now' also. This involves trusting in process and the universe of what is, 'here and now'. It is about having a connection with the other person, and goes beyond what

I see. Hence it is about the unseen dimension, which we cross over into when we shed this shell called a 'body'.

The spiritual nature of who I am is deep and intrinsic within this hologram model of Gestalt theory (diagram below). This is not seen at first glance, because one has to look deeper at what the theory is. There is, in the therapeutic relationship using the Gestalt approach, an alliance between client and therapist that develops when they come together and there is a connectedness of the 'I and Thou' through the dialogue, and being in the 'Here and Now' and staying with 'What and How' consolidates this.

This is described as a Hologram Model as each part of the hologram, and each part of gestalt therapy, contains the whole at the same time. So what we see below in the diagram is a two dimensional model of a four dimensional process.

Gestalt Hologram

Illawarra Gestalt Centre (O'Neill & O'Neill, 1995/2008)

Phenomenology

Awareness

"Here and now"

Dialogue/Existentialism

Contact/relationship

"I - thou"

Field theory

Connectedness

Authentic self"

Behaviourism

Experiment

"What and how"

KEY

Philosophy

Principle

"Practice"

When I work within this framework something happens that is not of a physical nature, and Hycner (1993, p 91) talks about these moments as being, "of a deep interpersonal meeting that takes us to the edge of the sacred" and if we attend to this he says, "they take us to a meeting with an otherness that touches us in our deepest being" and the magic happens at that moment.

Throughout history people have been searching for something more than what we see, know and understand. We have questions we want answered and there are so many diverse philosophies, doctrines, theories and beliefs to choose from and delve into to quench this thirst.

We have each collectively aligned ourselves with religions, organizations, beliefs and teachings to find these answers we search for. So many of us want to believe something more than what they see.

I could say Gestalt is my 'religion', but in saying this it would put Gestalt in just another box, and take away its uniqueness and I don't want to do that. Gestalt isn't a religion, there are no churches, ashrams, synagogues or temples in which to meet pray and share a common interest. There is no 'one' body that represents the whole in a physical sense. There is no 'one' text to draw from that 'one' can follow and get direction from.

Williams describes how -

> "We may discover that learning to experience spirit within a Gestalt (transpersonal) framework of awareness, openness, participation, relation, multidimensional, experience, and co-creation can lay the foundation for spiritual experience to emerge and therefore foster spiritual growth". (Vol 10, p. 15)

My experience of spirituality happens to me on a daily basis, some are more profound than others. Some are life changing like my marriage, the births of my two children and my divorce. Others are simple, like when I sit and appreciate the waves on a beach, the sand, the air, and the salt, and this is a joy and a mystery to me, a connection with nature.

As I obverse a new flower which has just bloomed in all its colour and glory, I am in awe. And to observe a child at play with all the innocence and beauty they exhibit, I feel love. When death occurs and I feel pain, loss, and anger, this too is a spiritual experience. Any situation I have been in, whether it was pleasant or unpleasant has been spiritual in nature for me and part of my journey in this life. As each day unfolds and then comes to a close, being alive and experiencing life on this continuum is for me having that spiritual experience.

Several years ago I received a phone call from a young man whose mother had passed away three years ago. He made an appointment to see me to address the grief he was experiencing from the loss. I knew it had taken a lot of courage to make that first phone call to me, for that initial appointment. I had been briefly acquainted with his mother when she was alive and known she and her son had shared a special bond.

That evening after the phone call I was moved to meditate. I asked the young man's mother to be present in the therapy room with us to be of support for her son and facilitate his healing. After the young man arrived for his session and we were half way through he began to smile. When I asked him what his smile meant he said to me 'you'll think I'm silly if I tell you'. I assured him there was nothing he could say in this room that was silly. He went on to tell me his mother was standing next to him in the room, and had been present for some time. He told me he often felt her presence with him and received much comfort from her.

I remember feeling an amazing sense of everything coming together, i.e. the physical, emotional, mental and spiritual. What happened in that room went out and beyond the realm of the physical. Everything seemed to stand still and I felt honoured to be in the presence of her 'spirit'. This experience once again shows me we live on a continuum of life-death-life.

Following on from that experience in the therapy room, I can relate to Stevens (1977) when he says "Gestalt is really more of a personal practice, a way of living, than it is a professional 'therapy' or 'cure'. It is something that you do with others, not to them". There was nothing I did during that session, other than be present and let the mystery take place of something bigger than myself.

In 1999 I was an intern at South Pacific Private (SPP), a rehabilitation centre in Sydney. It was there I was assigned to be with a Gestalt therapist for the duration of that period and as I sat in the therapy room I was introduced to and observed Gestalt Therapy in action as the therapist worked with her clients. I had never seen a therapist work in such a deep, respectful, and effective way in my life. This was a life changing experience for me, I had no idea this modality called Gestalt existed and that it would have a deep impact in my life.

After the third day at the Hospital I came home feeling very affected from what I had seen and experienced. I saw something rich and respectful in the Gestalt approach that moved me to my core, enough to know I needed to explore more about myself and how I am affected by myself and others, and how I affect them. Williams (Vol 10 2006) tells us how lots of people who have been involved in Gestalt therapy and training talk about their experiences as being "profound and spiritual in nature".

Working with clients in the therapeutic setting is having an alliance, a relationship, and not an environment where I fix them up. Crocker (1999) tells us "it is only oneself (in the environment) that can cure us", and it is in this I feel connected to myself and the other. This is for me another experience of the spiritual, and Zinker (1994) describes being fully present in a relationship as similar to, "worshipping together", and Crocker goes on to define spirituality as:

"The capacity to stand in the presence of a significant mystery and to respond to that spiritual reality in ways which honour it as the mystery it innately is." (Crocker, 1999, p. 310)

She says spiritual reality is something significant which is intrinsically neither fully knowable, fully controllable, nor fully predictable. Spiritual experiences carry with them the sense of being connected to some reality which is beyond the human person, and our experiences seem to go beyond ordinary sensory awareness, yet illuminate it and give meaning to it. She states the spiritual is not only deeply personal, but also transpersonal.

I believe the inclusion of the spiritual aspect within a modality is more dependent on the therapist than the model of therapy they practice. Crocker (1999) talks about the therapist using her own form of spirituality when she works with a client. She continues by saying that when a therapist is open to mystery she can honour that mystery which is not fully knowable, that element which cannot be controlled in the client.

In my twenties I was part of a Christian religion spreading the word of God to family and friends. There were times when I was involved in rituals of the church whereby I was euphoric and moved, and felt safe in the arms of God and the congregation. I loved to sing the psalms and 'praise the Lord'.

As time passed and my belief system and circumstances changed in my life, I moved away from the church and began exploring my beliefs without the confines and restrictions that a structured and organised church had bound me by. I became disillusioned by the control I saw men having over each other using their interpretation of the Bible to support what they said and did, and expectations for the congregation to conform.

I came to a realisation for myself that my spiritual side was not about religion and manmade organisations; it was about my connection to the wisdom of the universe, loving and being of service to mankind and nature. It was in this that my love laid.

In this new world of self-discovery I realised there was a smorgasbord of teaching's, beliefs and ways of being that

I could choose from, that would fit for me to operate authentically, without man-made groups defining how I should be. This was a continuation in my search for a more meaningful way I could be in this world. Crocker (1999) confirms this by saying "An authentically meaningful life can be lived only through the use of a cultivated spirituality". The more we know who we are, authentically, moves us closer to our spiritual nature. That experience almost 30 years ago was part of my journey to finally reaching the spirituality I experience today.

When I began my training at Illawarra Gestalt Centre (IGC), meeting and attending the training with thirteen other students was exciting, challenging and confronting. To expose my vulnerability weekend after weekend and sometimes leaving the centre feeling emotionally and physically ill was the best experience I could have had for my spiritual, personal, and educational growth. I looked at many parts of myself to heal the open emotional wounds I had with the support of facilitators and other students.

Then four years later as my training came to a close I recalled the many weekends I sat with my group of fourteen who I had shared my life, my secret fears, my vulnerability and this journey with, and they with me. I was faced with this being a closure of a part of my life and with these people that I would never see again together as my fellow colleagues in training at the Illawarra Gestalt Centre.

While I felt sadness and loss at this being an end, I also felt a renewal and a sense of completion. As this chapter was finishing a new chapter was beginning and I was aware of a growing excitement and exhilaration of new experiences and opportunities to expand myself and be better equipped to serve others. I wrote this poem for myself, and fellow students remembering what we had shared together.

Hearts connected in
A Sun drenched space
Open and taken to a
Vulnerable place
Our group has evolved now
To be who we are
An imprint in our hearts
Whether near or afar

Some clients don't have a spiritual belief and wouldn't be interested in my view as a therapist to bring that into their sessions. What is spirituality to one person may not be the same for another, depending on their interpretation, so I am mindful and respectful of the 'other' in life to keep what is mine, mine and will share that part only if invited.

Sue Murray (1995, p.11) says "some clients will be quite happy with where they are and what they are doing and the spiritual isn't important, or they have a spiritual understanding that doesn't need dealing with in the therapy room."

Conclusion

I have shared with you what my spirituality is and I have conveyed also that Gestalt is part of my spiritual daily practice. I have created a life for myself that consists of love, contentment, peace and a caring of myself in a way that even when life is difficult and challenging I know something better waits for me at the end of this journey of life. By incorporating some of my own experiences I have shown there is a thread to link Gestalt to my practice of spirituality.

I hope you have enjoyed reading this article about my spiritual nature and what that means to me. I want to say thank you to my trainers and fellow trainees for my four years of training that have sent me in a new wonderful direction of motivation, self discovery, and more personal growth.

Kahuna Body Work

by

Sara Gylany

"An ancient spiritual healing art
reclaimed from the field."

*Kahuna is a word that's come to mean
different things in its translation from
Hawaiian language to western usage.
Used randomly such as in the movie The
Big Kahuna with Kevin Spacey about
salesmen and the meaning of life, to Gold
Coast ice cream parlours offering pineapple
flavoured "Kahuna" treats!*

I am a Cultural Bodyworker (*Kahuna, Maori, Aboriginal healing arts*) and a Gestalt therapist. For the last seven years while continuing my own personal growth journey I have been practicing and providing my clients with a combination of Gestalt therapy but predominantly "kahuna" bodywork.

The Kahunas were men and women held in high esteem at a time when whole oceanic communities relied upon them for their well-being and survival. The Kahunas both inherited and learned useful and sacred knowledge based on universal laws for health, happiness and sustainable living. They were specialists in fields such as navigation, building, medicine, food, counseling, healing and temple priests. The lineage of Kahunas was nearly lost, driven underground and banned from practicing, initially by missionaries from New England who wanted to establish churches on the islands to "save the savages" from themselves.

Then came industry, immigration and war to the Hawaiian Islands and these Pacific Island peoples with their open hearted and apparently simple approach to life, were more often than not ignored, suppressed or consumed by this influx of Western ways of being. Their spirituality and medicines were brushed aside leaving them unable to prevent, much less accommodate, the new ideas, lifestyle, foods and diseases from engulfing their lands.

In my view it is none to soon that their traditional, more inclusive spiritual and holistic approaches to health and well-being are being reclaimed. Kahuna is based on Huna psychology which emphasizes "right relationship" to self and environment. I believe it is a profoundly simple ethic to assist in our planets survival and evolution. It's said a country and culture is shaped by the language and visa versa. The Hawaiian language is a beautiful and lyrical language and I have little knowledge of the complex and multi-layered interpretation of their language. What little I have learnt about the word "kahuna" is it can be written as Ka Huna, Kahuna and kahuna. It is fairly widely known there that the word Huna means "secret"- hidden or unconscious and this term refers to the traditional Hawaiians philosophy for life.

Kahuna is a title earned or handed down to a person and translates to "keeper of the secrets". I also know that "kahuna" bodywork (as used in the western world) refers to a training and healing massage or bodywork style with a strong focus on the metaphysical and "right relationship". A sacred and ceremonial healing art, practiced mainly in their temples built for practicing "right relationship" with God/Source and the kings and queens who ruled the communities. and *not* (as massage can be defined in the West) as an invitation to distort or use as euphemism for sexual gratification or the pervert-factor.!

It was suggested I write about my own kahuna bodywork (spiritual) practice when I was asked at a workshop as to what actually *happens* in a kahuna session. I do feel passionately about "earth based" traditional and indigenous healing practices and I feel connected to the broader field when I write about what I do for work as a healing therapist. Learning and practicing earth-based traditional healing arts brings back balance to the world for me, in a world where something akin to intellectual worship and specifically western medical science worship, persists. The left-brain-rationalising and analysing mind dominates when it comes to our well-being and medical choices. I believe we've forgotten how to intuit or trust the body to give us signals and natural solutions to our ills and stresses.

Interestingly I also experience Gestalt therapy like the kahuna healing that is to say, holistic, present-centered and inclusive of body *and* mind for growth and process. Both are "field" oriented or (acknowledging the influence

88

of the unseen or past and future processes). Each attends to the whole person, body, mind and soul or spirit. Similarly both trainings provided me with experiences of initiation or a process of transition into deeper ways of being. Kahuna bodywork is a style of massage and healing that can bring awareness to the mind, as insight or understanding about any underlying belief patterns or emotions "held" in the body as twitches, pain or stiffness. The bodywork along with awareness can release or unlock feelings held in the muscles, joints and even deeper to the cells themselves!

There is a yogic teaching that every breath and every thought has a vibration often called energy or *prana*. And this vibration affects each and every cell in the body. So too, kahuna training teaches us to work with that energy level, to tune in and intuit which area needs attention or find out by asking the client "what's coming up for you" around a particular area on the body. Also, to connect with the outer energy field, which surrounds the body and from which all energy flows. A continuous, connected cycle, which can be hindered or blocked when life doesn't flow quite smoothly. Kahuna bodywork helps reconnect that flow cycle along the meridian channels (part of the body's natural healing system). The bodywork focus is to help align body, mind and spirit, connecting to the energy field and focusing here and now, centering in the heart— where it is believed the soul resides. I use the word "field" to refer not only to the body's unseen energy fields, but also as in Gestalt therapy's "field theory" or organism/environment field. The field is that which surrounds and flows through all life forms—it is the now, the tomorrow, the yesterday, the stillness and the chaos. This is the "between" of person and their environment; the context in which experiences are experienced, the spaces where our stories unfold. It is the "between" energy that happens when relating and present for another, Buber's *I and Thou.* (1970)

Pacific Island cultures and specifically the Hawaiian Islands indigenous peoples with their Huna psychology refer to this unseen but felt "field" phenomena. Huna evolved over centuries of observation and living within the natural environment. In the human body this energy or field is called *mana,* or life force. An energy source we take in from the food we eat, the air we breath, the water we drink and the thoughts we have. It is our connection to Source. In Huna they say the only path to God or Source is through right and proper relationships here on earth, and most importantly not having thoughts or actions which harm another. They teach three levels of consciousness (lower, middle and higher selves) and God as a triune being or a trinity of levels of Spirit. To become at-one with God was through the Higher Self (in alignment with lower and middle self) and right living.

Huna may be one of the oldest "psychologies" on the planet and is pragmatic and holistic. Our industrialised world with economic rationalism and the tendency to split holistic systems into dualities or opposites has separated us from our own selves and our connection to or within a field. The examples are endless, men/women, mind/body, religion/nature, conqueror/conquered, symptom/cause, conventional medicine/natural medicine. Huna and kahuna body healing encourages awareness of the whole in a universal context. It also taps into the body's innate self-healing mechanism. Trusting the organism as a process and in process, rather than a fixed or stagnant disease-destined biology, that will only respond to synthetic drugs or life-saving (and sometimes *not*) surgery or invasive medicine.

Kahuna based health is thought of more as a state of mind aligned with body and spirit, an aligning process which can be assisted sometimes by surgery, medicine including synthetic drugs or Island, Ayervedic, Chinese, European medicine plus *alive*, healthy food/nutrition and right relationship. Kahuna bodywork I feel, has something to add to the mix of massage modalities. On the physical level it's the flowing movements over the body, reconnecting energy flows, meridians/ chi channels and stimulating healthy functioning of internal organs. This alone can make us *feel* great. It also holds a bigger-picture intent. By this I mean an intent or focus of mind that connects to the energy beyond the physical. Connecting that energy-thought or intent to the flow of energy *through* the practitioners heart to the clients energy field. One of those "right relationships" really.

It can also assist a person through emotional and mental transitions. By supporting the person to be present, in their body with what is, the kahuna bodyworkers working in Hawaiian temples could have many practitioners working on one body to nurture and "hold" energies within the body and from the field, and thus assisting a person through a healing crisis or through transition from one state of mind to another. It was sacred and ceremonial work. Understanding that it is the "field" or Source which heals, the practitioner is the conduit. With kahuna bodywork, slightly different from lomi lomi (where the hands are predominantly used with flowing movements) the whole forearm is the surface used to contact the skin and massage with oil. (Some bodywork is also done on a clothed body and on floor mats.) The forearms "pick up" blocked energy and "sweep" or encourage the system to release toxins (mental and physical!) along the forearms and "out" of the hands. In particular a *Cultural Bodywork* which is Kahuna infused with Maori & Aboriginal healing arts, brings a powerful feeling of groundedness to all that "energy" work. The emphasis is also on "right" relationship between practitioner and client, with connection maintained throughout, albeit in silence through touch or intention.

Our training mantra goes like this:

THE KAHUNA WAY

Today not tomorrow
Now not later
No discussion
Just do it.
You need to be logical sometimes
And Brave others.

Everything is Connected

Everything is together

They are placed together Connected

This is Kahuna

Present

All is Connected

To understand Kahuna you must carry it

Into every moment of your life

Once everything that feeds you is

Connected then you are in a flow

Connected

I love the "work" and working with the body in this sacred way. I find it most healing and helpful for clients wishing to unravel issues or just to rest and regenerate, returning to themselves, their inner wisdom, here and now. This, to me, is Kahuna Bodywork, and by the *infusion* of Cultural bodywork, is the way I try to live and work with spirit - through these ancient teachings of the Pacific Islands and Oceanic healing and knowledge.

A Journey through Mourning

by

Seán Gaffney

In memory of my son, Dara Gaffney

May 9, 1972 – August 9, 1986

Allow me to begin with some extracts from the interview by Belinda Harris, published in the British Gestalt Journal (Gaffney, 2008), which started me off on the reflections described in this article:

Belinda: *I'll start with a personal question, Seán. What brought you to gestalt therapy? Why gestalt for you, at whatever point in your life it was?*

Seán: *There are probably two answers, or one answer embedded in the other. Mm. In fact, I first clearly understood and publicly acknowledged their connection only a few days ago, at Charlie Bowman's pre-conference workshop on the history of gestalt therapy, which included our own histories as practitioners. So my answer begins in my earlier life, when before my 18th birthday I entered a Cistercian monastery and felt completely at home. I really, really felt it. But before my two year novice period was up my novice master, Father Ambrose, called me and said 'I've been thinking a lot about you, brother, and you don't belong here. You're a teacher, a communicator. If you really want to be a priest be a preacher but the contemplative life is just a waste of your talents.'*

I have described this experience in the first issue of Inner Sense (Gaffney 2007). It has become more and more formative for me as I look back on my life, and now more clearly connected to the topic of this article: a journey through mourning and the meaning of a life...

Seán: *Anyway, to get back to answering your question about what brought me to Gestalt therapy: the second and more formal, rational answer would be: In 1986 my youngest son died of leukaemia. He went very, very quickly, exactly two months and one week from diagnosis to death...*

And later in the interview:

My dead son is involved here somewhere in another, more directly influential way. One of the things I did as a consequence of that period around his death and his mother's obvious painful grieving was to decide' 'I'm going to become a better person. I probably wasn't the best father in the world; I probably favoured his big brother more. I clearly wasn't a good support to my wife. I've got to be a better person. I need to do something to be a better person'. When I graduated from the Gestalt Academy of Scandinavia and the group of us were sitting there I said, 'Thanks to my son, I promised myself to be a better person, and thanks to these four or five years I believe I'm becoming one"

So let me now, after a brief detour into the safer territory of quoted references, go straight to the point: shortly after the fourteenth birthday of my youngest of two sons, he became ill, with very diffuse symptoms. I took him to our local clinic, where the diagnosis was an infection of some sort, with prescribed antibiotics and a week's rest. He appreciated the week off school, though did not seem to be getting over his symptoms of tiredness, mild though diffuse pain, and a general listlessness. Despite his prescribed freedom with no school and no homework, he showed little interest in TV or videos.

On June 1, 1986, he had severe pain, mainly in his stomach. His mother – a social worker student and a part-time assistant nurse – took him to the emergency ward at our local hospital, where she herself worked. I was away, teaching. My wife phoned me that evening to say that Dara had been immediately transferred to the cancer ward of the Children's Hospital, which, she knew, was the leukaemia ward.

I returned immediately and went to visit him. He was clearly unwell and in pain. My wife was very concerned, using her experience in the hospital and conversations with the nursing staff. I was...well, optimistic is the wrong word. Maybe re-assured that he was in a good hospital and with my belief that treatment worked.

Two days later, my wife and I had a meeting with his doctor, a soft-spoken and gentle man originally from northern Africa. He declared the diagnosis – acute myelocetic leukaemia – and spoke of the chemotherapy treatment that would start immediately and continue for about two or up to three months. If the cancer was arrested then, it would be time to maybe start looking at such interventions as a bone marrow transplant and he would need to start taking samples to establish who would be a suitable donor, probably our oldest son. He was clear about the statistics: 60% chance of improvement, 40% chance of moving into a terminal condition. For this particular form of leukaemia, the average for Sweden (population 8.5 million) was four cases per year.

My son was in the leukaemia ward on the eighth floor of the children's hospital. The ninth floor had been adapted for parents and relatives to spend nights there in order to be near their children. My wife and I took a room there so that one of us at least would always be around, day and night, using a shift system on weekdays, and staying there for most of the weekend. My wife and I re-arranged our work schedules so that we could attend to both our sons.

Reflecting back to this period, I am now more aware than I was then of the differences in how my wife and I heard and interpreted the information we regularly received. For her, the doctor was preparing us for the worst. For me, he was keeping us informed of progress without making any promises. She became more and more withdrawn, at times impossible to reach in any way that I knew how. We became more distanced from each other, sometimes only meeting briefly as we took over from each other at the hospital. The few hours we might be at home with our other son, we did the practical things together that had to be done and otherwise kept our exchanges to a social minimum.

As we moved through July, it was becoming increasingly difficult to distinguish between the impact of his leukaemia and the impact of the chemotherapy on Dara's condition. His immune system was degraded by the treatment and he was susceptible to heavy colds, sudden fevers, exhaustion, complete loss of appetite, and days which he slept through from one to the next.

By the end of July, a mere two months after admission to the hospital, his condition was worsening on a daily basis. All talk of a bone marrow transplant was now out of the question. The personnel moved an extra bed into Dara's room so that my wife and I could choose to sleep there with him in his room. I slept there the three last nights of his short life. My wife was working nights during this time, dropped in to see him during the night, and slept at home during the daytime.

When I awoke on the morning August 9, 1986, Dara was asleep, breathing shallowly and his whole body burning hot with fever. There was an intern on duty that morning and I asked him to check on my son and tell me what was happening. He asked me where my wife was. I told him that she was at home, sleeping.

"I think you better call her, and get her here" he said. I did, and she came. We were at our son's bedside when he died, early that afternoon.

Our eldest boy, Naoise, was on his way back from Ireland that same day. Because of very strained relations between my wife and my family in Dublin, none of us had been back to Ireland since coming to Sweden, 11 years earlier. Naoise was a dedicated scout and troop leader, and, the previous year, his troop had planned a study visit to Ireland in the first week of August, ending this very day. I had earlier phoned a close friend of mine and told him of the situation. With an amazing effort and great ingenuity, he had traced Naoise to the harbour where he was waiting to board the ferry. With the help of the ferry personnel and scout leaders, Naoise was put in a taxi and was on his way to Dublin Airport with a flight booked by my friend back to Stockholm where he would be met and brought straight to the hospital.

His brother died while all this was happening. The ward staff arranged for Dara's body to be brought to the hospital chapel so that Naoise could say his farewell when he arrived later that evening.

(Months later, Naoise told me that he had spoken with Dara about the trip to Ireland and his own willingness to stay in Sweden. I was amazed and moved to hear that Dara had spoken of possibly dying, and that he did not want to deprive his brother of a trip that was so important to him. If he went, and Dara died, then Naoise would anyway have been back to Ireland and met their cousins, whom Dara did not remember – he was two years old when we moved to Sweden. If he didn't go, and Dara died, then this would always be between them.)

As is common in Sweden and a shock to me, the funeral was to be some 10 days later. My wife reminded me of a christening we had attended at the Catholic church in central Stockholm, where we had both been impressed by the priest, a German Jesuit whose name I got from the father of the christened child – Pater Peter Hornung. I phoned the church and found myself speaking with Pater Hornung for almost an hour. I could feel and sense his care, gentleness and warmth.

A few days later, my wife and I met Pater Hornung. "My name is Peter Hornung", he said, "that's 'honung' with an 'r'". 'Honung' is Swedish for honey...(right now, in mid-sentence, I think of Karen Horney, the psychoanalyst, also 'honey' with an 'r'). We spent almost an afternoon with him in what was a gentle combination of counselling, pastoral care, and the practicalities of our son's funeral. Amongst these was the hard practicality of our family not being parishioners, and our son not formally baptised. This meant that we could not have a full church funeral. What Pater Hornung proposed was that we have a private funeral in the chapel at the Catholic section of our local cemetery – located directly in view of the balconies on the eighth and ninth floors of the children's hospital – and a memorial mass, which he would celebrate, the Saturday after the funeral, in the church.

My wife attended the funeral, and not the mass. Pater Hornung had suggested that we bring some of Dara's favourite music with us. I remembered him telling me once, with a young teenager's earnestness, that Annie Lennox of Eurythmics was the best singer in the world. I prepared a tape with her singing "I walk into an empty room/And suddenly my heart goes boom - There must be an angel/Playing with my heart". Annie Lennox was for my son; today, I can realise that the song was for me. Since then, I still can't hear it without opening up to my memories, or closing down in a non-supportive environment, knowing that I can raise the song again later and be open to its influence.

I still and often remember that mass. I had put an announcement in the Deaths column of the main newspapers and was amazed to find the church absolutely full. Almost all of the Swedes, including classmates, teachers, neighbours, family friends had a flower with them to place on the non-existent coffin, having confused the memorial mass with a funeral. Pater Hornung noticed this and immediately said that he would stop at an appropriate moment during the mass to allow these flowers to be placed on the altar, which he did.

When it was time for his sermon, he stood silently on the side of the altar, looked up and around and said words I have never forgotten. I am convinced as I write that what follows is more verbatim than it is a paraphrase:

"At a time like this, when we remember a fourteen year old boy, some may wonder about the meaning of life. What is the meaning of Dara's life? I can tell you his meaning for me, who never met him and who buried his dead body. YOU are the meaning of his life to me. Here I am, a German Jesuit, a missionary and a parish priest, speaking to a church full of...non-practicing Catholics, since I recognise nobody; Lutherans in name though maybe not in practice; agnostics, atheists, humanists...and more besides. This is a dream come true for me – thanks to Dara, whose life made this possible. The meaning of Dara's life is not what he achieved or failed at in his fourteen years. The meaning of his life is in the influence of his life and death on us he leaves behind, and on how open we are to allowing that meaning be a part of our lives as we go on living. If we forget him, then his life and death become meaningless to us."

There was a long silence as he finished and returned to complete the mass.

****

Allow me here to return to the BGJ interview, where I summarise the immediate and subsequent events:

In 1986 my youngest son died of leukemia. He went very, very quickly, exactly two months and one week from diagnosis to death. This totally threw me. One of the many consequences of this was that my wife completely crumbled and eventually was diagnosed with paranoid schizophrenia, and because of the complications of the medical system in Sweden there was no way in which she could be prescribed treatment, or helped unless she agreed to it - or I threw her out, if I literally put her outside the door and phoned the authorities and said there's a person with grave difficulties, somebody homeless outside my door, then they would come.

I actually had this debate with various authorities. At the same time she was and is the mother of our oldest son. So there was a period when I was living in an apartment with my wife who was becoming my ex-wife, because in the middle of all this she divorced me, and my son who had lost his little brother. The circumstances were extremely demanding. One of the consequences of my wife's condition was that she reversed day and night totally. So she was up all night and slept all day so everything was chaotic, there were always separate lives being lived completely out of sync in this small apartment. Eventually after much maneuvering and in cooperation with her former employer – the hospital where she worked part-time and where our son had died...eventually, they managed to create a situation where they could pro-actively take care of an employee and arranged for a period in a kind of residential treatment centre.

That created a situation where there was a little bit of space, so I had a grieving process going on for myself, and supporting my son, my ex-wife who now was clearly in the middle of a very severe grieving process...

****

I had started writing poetry in my very early teens, in both English and Gaelic, and have continued ever since, though nowadays in English and Swedish. I have only ever published three – two in English and one in Swedish. One of the two in English accompanied the BGJ interview. It was my celebration of Dara's 21st anniversary. I say "celebration" in the sense that every recognition of his influence on my life is indeed a celebration of the meaning of his life. So – yes, a celebration, no matter how much sorrow or regret or shame each poem expresses, or humour or joy. These poems, over a period now of 22 years, have become my "Journey Through Mourning", with all its ambiguity.

Over the years, these poems have simply emerged, sometimes complete, sometimes in parts over a day or days or even weeks. I became used to being open for a line to emerge, and, when it sounded, tasted, felt "right", I would see what followed. I have committed few of them to paper until they were finished in my body.

My intention here is to select from them as I, for the first time publicly, explore my mourning and its meaning with the poems as my guide. The only changes I have made for publication are concerned with clarity, never content. This selection is intended to capture the main themes which have emerged over the past 22 years, and will include my first and my most recent poem.

The first one came within days of Dara's death. Someone had asked me, in Swedish, how I was. Directly translated, this particular phrase would be "How is it?" This became the opening line of my first, unexpected poem:

1.

there is nothing it is like.
it is. it
is the gaps we leave still in our conversations.

is your place at the table empty but
still set sometimes and unset again.

is the rocking chair you'd sit in, observing
sat in by someone the day of your funeral
shock of him sitting on top of you there.

the gaps we leave still in our conversations
the place beside me at the table empty
rocking chair you'd sit in, observing
shock of you not sitting there to observe us.

there is nothing it is like.

it is all of these and more of them and none of them.

it is.

This first poem was a flower that bloomed in the wasteland of my life at that time. It opened and its seeds blew within me. Soon poems began forming spontaneously in me, and I processed them until each was finished, ended, temporarily complete. I say "temporarily", since some poems and lines re-emerged in later pieces. One theme which has never left me came in the second poem, which, in itself, was an echo of the first one:

2.

you will always be not here.
your birthdays will be would have beens,
at would have been twenty one you will be
unimaginable.
at would have been eighteen you will be
unimaginable.

at would have been fifteen you will be
fourteen still

fourteen years and three months to the day
killed by leukaemia.

you are not.
there is no you.
you are a he that was
and not a you even.
you are a he that was.
you were and are my son and I miss you not here now,
not
ever.
again.
here.

My anger was a theme that emerged early and changed form over time: as I select poems now, I find I am re-visiting the times and places of their creation, and the emotions I was experiencing then – and now again, though softer.

4.

leukaemia is a cruel and brutal killer
gnawed and gnashed in you
sucked sickly at the marrow in your bones

polluted you
even the treatment
polluted you

pushed the hair out from under your burning skin
pushed your food back out through your sore filled mouth
gushed shit out of your seeping anus

sickness and treatment
polluting you
killing you

cruelly
brutally
killing you

and all our matter of fact trivialities
our let's be practical delusions
our crying won't help him helplessness our
may the end come quickly never despair

cruelly
brutally
killing you

This poem re-appeared soon after as a variation on the same theme explicitly repeated. I remember how the ending differed with a new theme emerging, though I had no real idea of this at the time:

9.
even the treatment
polluted him
sickness and treatment
polluting him

killing him
cruelly
brutally
killing him

this repetition a release and a reminder:

I'll exorcise his dying not
your life your life
lives on in me

Another theme was around our family:

7.

we are a square
collapsed to a triangle
one corner gone and
half our space our
distances distorted

On the night of the funeral, my wife moved out of our bedroom into Dara's room and bed. The following day, she nailed up double blankets over the window and kept the room in total darkness. Two weeks later, she was sent home from her work. I had no idea of the details at the time, and only caught glimpses of them later. One thing I learned later was that she was regarded as being on sick leave. This led to a period at home of extreme stress and unpredictability. It is only since becoming a gestalt therapist myself that I was able to see perspectives that were beyond me at the time. Amongst the stresses were occasional brief and sharp outbursts by my wife, accusing my family of things which were partly recognisable, and partly imaginary. These outbursts were also directed at me, including my inadequacies as a father to Dara: how I never loved him

113

as much as Naoise, how I didn't take his illness seriously, how my grieving for him was inadequate and typical of the selfish person I was.

In the midst of all this, my wife sought a divorce and only needed my signature for it to become a formality, three months later. In the circumstances, I admit, with some shame, that I was relieved at the time. Her divorcing me would be one problem less to deal with. My focus was fully on both of my sons, one dead, his big brother living in a home that was fast becoming a hell. I am remembering the insoluble dilemmas I was facing: grieving for Dara, with all the shame and guilt I felt; supporting my living son, not only in his own loss of his little brother, for whom he had always been a big brother – with all that entails - but also protecting my son from an insufferable situation at home. And protecting myself from the increasingly disjointed accusations of my wife, now my ex-wife but still living in the family home...though the family was truly collapsed in on itself.

Earlier, on my wife's initiative – she was studying to be a social worker - we had all four started in family therapy (psychodynamic) some six months previously. My wife had dropped out, following an argument with the two therapists. I and the two boys continued. Then Dara was invited to join a group of his own age. Then Naoise was invited to move to the Youth Department, which he did, and I stayed in therapy on my own.

After Dara's death and the subsequent events at home, I too dropped out and Naoise continued. So I had a sense that he had a place to get support. My self-support was in dealing with the situation at home, getting back to work as a lecturer – and managing my constant grief. Divorce seemed like a way out. What I had not understood was that my wife – soon formally my ex-wife – had no intention of moving from our apartment. So for a further six months the three of us lived this strange, disjointed, disconnected life in the same space and times...

Throughout this confusing time, poems continued to emerge. My guilt and shame were themes which bloomed and spread their seeds:

8.

cold fact of your absence crying through my mind

tears of my thoughts freeze and craze in me
my dry eyes pain with the hurt behind them

my memory cringes with images of your suffering

something inside me shrivels at
thoughts of my thoughtlessness:

the hug I needed the hug I gave you your skin
screaming at the contact:

daddy, daddy please
daddy!
daddy!

more confusion than anger
an appeal more than anger
an appeal not to hurt you

I think of you begging me your father not to hurt you
images of your suffering
images of my clumsiness

Dara, Dara please
Dara!
Dara!
teach me your meaning

During this first of my twenty two years of
mourning, there were moments when my sorrow met

joyful memories and these themes intertwined, weaving strangely integrated patterns of polarities:

10.
sometimes I see you.

my lips forms your words in my head:

I-HAVE-NO-HOMEWORK-OKAY?
I-HAVE-NO-HOMEWORK.
YOU relax at the weekend
YOU go to the bloody bookshops
spend all day just looking at books

SO: I. HAVE. NO. HOMEWORK.
OKAY? OKAY?

so can I go out now to my friends
smirking and smiling your triumph at me...

or:

mew – mew – mew – mew – SEEK
mimicking my stammer and my clumsy Swedish
mew – mew – mewssssSEEK

say it again daddy say it again
mewmewmew
it's so funny daddy: say it again!

or:

Daddy Daddy please
Daddy!
Daddy!

18.
I'm learning to laugh again
good-hearted chuckles bubbling up from in me

Sometimes when I meet you where we've been before
I hear you clearly begging me:

Tell it again daddy please
daddy daddy tell it again
it's so funny
daddy daddy please come on daddy

You could hear the same joke twenty times and laugh
each time equally heartily
your eyebrows up under your quiff

mouth opening to welcome the punchline
helplessly creasing yourself giggling and laughing

Sometimes I meet you where we'll never be
hear you sometimes where you can't be now
know it's anyway you I'm seeing
know it must be you I'm hearing –

hear you giggling watch your mouth opening
a t.v programme maybe or your granddad's latest bargain

or something I hear of I know you'd laugh at
or something I think of I know you'd laugh at

share it with you say to someone who knew you
Dara would have laughed at that

Dara would laugh at that I say
learning again to laugh at it with you

19.
hairs in the bathtub
mine or your brother's

hairs in the bathtub remind me

moulting, your insides mangy with poisons

hair everywhere strands and clumps of it

so we shaved your head
crossed a border into no-man's-land
burned your bridges though we didn't say so

you wanted a wig but you never wore it

out for those royal tours in your wheelchair
you lifting your hat to old ladies passing
laughed baldly when we'd passed them said
stop stop quick wait here's another one ready?

bald bony dying still you

A theme which re-emerged and has followed me is the confusion of Dara's birthday. This more than anything is an annual reminder of his death, of the end of his life, the end of our physical time together.

14.

today you are would-have-been fifteen

at five i think it was twenty five
five twenty five p.m Irish time
fifteen years ago today you were born

today you are nine months dead
at 14.50 Swedish time
nine months ago today you died

the nurses didn't let me see you born

the nurses let me see you dying
the nurses let me see you die

today at 14.50 you are nine months dead
at 17.25 then would have been fifteen

i'll first relive your dying then

A number of other themes had emerged during this first year after Dara's death, all somehow flattened by his absence as evoked by his would-have-been-fifteen-day and now the powerful finality of his first anniversary:

121

25,

this night last year the last night of your life

this night last year the first night of this year

i didn't know then you were dying then

you'd asked to have the extra bed back in
this week last year the last week of your life

my turn to sleep there in your room that night
this night last year the first night of this year

i didn't know then you were dying then

i knew that you were dying but not that then i mean
this night last year the last night of your life

i didn't know then you were dying then

this night last year the first night of this year

this night last year the last night of your life

There was a dreadful finality about Dara's first anniversary. A Christmas come and gone without his subtle signals and delight. A birthday come and gone and still the same age as on the day of his death. An anniversary confirming the obvious – Dara was dead and always would be, for the rest of my life. And somehow, dead but not gone and not forgotten. I understood that the meaning of his short life for me would be in how I remembered him and gave his life meaning for me through how his influence lived on in me.

For most of this first year, I felt as if I were living in a number of parallel worlds. I was absorbed by my grieving, grabbing private moments to ponder my sorrow, my guilt, my shame, my memories of Dara and his life with me, and mine with him, and mostly expressed in the poems which just kept coming. My home life was in chaos. Naoise needed more support than I could give him, and I was truly grateful that he was still in therapy. My work as a lecturer had lost much of its excitement for me – it had become a job, a way of paying the bills. My one good friend, Terry, from Wales, whose family and ours had socialised a lot together, became the channel for my feelings, and I could just let go of whatever was going on for me in his attentive company.

And then, of course, another year without Dara had started:

Sixt....
a month to go today until your
would-have-been-sixteen day

(this month I know is April and my watch says ninth)

four months to go today until your
second anniversary

(the month will then be August and my watch says ninth)

is sixteen worse than fifteen – if so why?
and first one worse than second – if so why?

surely your absence cannot match your presence
surely your life is worth more than your death:
I'll write this for you now not then:
you were you are – not would-have-been

Early in the Autumn term of 1987, I found myself at a Training and Development Exhibition as part of my work. A woman stepped out from a stand as I rushed past and asked: "Are you in crisis?" "Do you want to change?" "Yes and yes", I replied She handed me a leaflet for a 3 X 4-day Gestalt residential. By the end of this residential, I felt that I had come home in some way. I applied to the Gestalt Academy of Scandinavia for their 4–year Diploma Programme in Gestalt Therapy. I started in August, 1988, two years after Dara's death. I had understood that even if I never became a "better" person, I could at least open myself to change.

Some pieces from this period:

May 19, 1990

at would-have-been-eighteen today
you are not with me now

you were and are and always will be
fourteen years and three months to the day
All Souls' Day, 1991
I light a candle for each of you:
My granddad, my father and my son.

You, granddad, thought I could be your son
Heard in my voice your dead son's echo...

You, my father, just never knew how to be one
Hoped you could be one if I became your son.

And you, my son, hoped I would be your father.
And now I'm learning how to be your son.

I stand here last of our four generations
Alive in the lives of you, my special dead.

May 9, 1991

Dear Dara,
okay, okay :I'm still not really good:
but you will agree I'm changing.
so: thanks for being you,
thanks for your patience.
love,
Daddy

I completed my training in May, 1992. I can see now, as I write this sentence, that I started the month of his death, and finished the month of his birth. Between his dying and his birth...That summer, I attended a 4-

day residential Psychosynthesis retreat, where the following poem emerged:

Siljan-song
On a hill above Lake Siljan I give myself an hour
And watch the trees around me being trees;
And watch the grass around me being grass;
And see each bush, plant, weed and flower.

On a hill above Lake Siljan I give myself the time
To see ants, busy, on a mottled stone;
To hear each birdsong, separate, distinct;
To sit here, waiting for a rhyme.

On a hill above Lake Siljan, I'm happy to just be,
Accepting all the ups and downs I've had,
Accepting all the paths that lie ahead:
On a hill above Lake Siljan, I'm learning to be me.

On the first anniversary of Dara's death, I established a ritual which became obsessive. First, a visit to the florists at the cemetery entrance close to the Catholic graveyard, where I bought two potted white wild daisy plants, and two protected candles. I would then go the chapel where we held the funeral service, and plant the daisies and light a candle at the small mound opposite the chapel with a crucifix. After some time there, I would walk to the hill on which the Memorial Garden was, where Dara's ashes had been strewn. Here I would again plant daisies and light a candle and reflect. I did this for fourteen years.

And then came Dara's fourteenth anniversary. I can remember sobbing and shaking with tears as I sat by the chapel and realized he was now dead as long as he had been alive. Still sobbing, I walked to the Memorial Garden. I sobbed and moaned with grief. Suddenly, I was stilled, then exhilarated: I did not need any empty rituals to commemorate him. My life was my commemoration. My work at opening to change. My work at being a good father to his brother, Naoise. All that I did to give meaning to his life through the influence of his life and death on me, and, through me, on others: my therapy clients, my training groups, my supervisees, my university students – all had Dara to thank for any value they found in working with me. I walked laughing down the hill, and have not been back there since.

Since then, my only "ritual" is to keep the days around his anniversary completely free, and also to celebrate his birthday. I never know how I will be impacted, simply that I will be, in one way or another.

And the poems still came, old themes returning, new ones poking up like wild flowers, all becoming perfect parts of a colourful bouquet of celebration. This process over the twenty two years since his death can be captured in the two most recent anniversary poems:

1
you are twenty one years dead today.
twenty.
one.
years.

dead.
today and then i saw you die and see you die again.

i stood and stand now by your bedside.
my finger touched and touches now the heat of your hand.
i did not touch you more than that, it caused you pain.

your startled wide-eyed stare.
your startled wide-eyed stare a shift and you were gone.
i dared to touch your burning hand.
you neither moved nor sounded.

you are twenty one years dead today.
and now again I dare to touch your burning hand.
i take your hand to guide us through this day.

2

my guilt my shame my sorrow and
the black hole of your absence:
forever fourteen.
your brother now a man of thirty seven.
forever fourteen.

and me with two weeks now to sixty five.
and you are still
forever fourteen

still
the black hole of your absence all these years.

This was as cathartic an experience as was that of his fourteenth anniversary, though fundamentally different. In the first, I went from helpless grief, shame and guilt into the joy of discovering that Dara was in me and with me, not in a chapel or a Memorial Garden. On his twenty first anniversary, his death and total physical absence from my life hit me deeply.

He was not with me in my life now as a 35 year-old man. He had been missing physically from my life for 21 years, though always a presence as a permanent 14 year-old, fixed and frozen in time. The Autumn which followed was a strange period, of mild depression, loneliness, and reflection.

The summer of 2008 became special for me. The interview with Belinda Harris came as a total surprise in terms of its theme – a personal portrait – and the pathways on which Belinda and I wandered. I had never before been so public about Dara's death and its influence on my becoming a Gestalt therapist. I spent the week following the interview in Belfast with three good friends, among them Brian O'Neill, originally from Belfast.

I met members of his family there as well as four delightful young children on the street where we were staying, and who were convinced that I was Santa Claus on a trial trip to the Falls Road area, checking it out for Christmas...they sang "Jingle Bells" for me. Seventeen times in a raucous row and I enjoyed every minute of it.

These children then came to talk with me every time I stepped out onto the street for a cigarillo. I became aware of how much I enjoyed their presence and how open I was to their endless questions. Not at all the self-importantly impatient and busy person I could often be with Dara during his lifetime.

I returned to Sweden, where I live, and then went down to my isolated house in the country as the anniversary approached. A poem emerged in the usual way: an opening line that clicked into place and the rest simply followed. I had it clean and clear in my head before I wrote it down. Here it is:

August 9, 2008
1.
awaiting you to rise in me again
ready as always to meet you when you come

meet you sometimes where we've been before and
places where you've never been I think you'd like
I meet you and I feel you smile and nod

and always and forever fourteen

I celebrate your birthday every year

your deathday too
always and forever fourteen

2.
something is changing for us now

I started fixing place and day
never to forget you:

the chapel where your funeral was with
annie lennox singing of an angel

the hillock where your ashes
whitened the wild grass then
washed by rain absorbed by the wet earth

and always august ninth

and then that day when you were
fourteen years dead

fourteen years living and now
fourteen years dead

sharp painful flamed epiphany
cauterized my wounds

I came there dulled with grieving and regret
and left in joy

those places unimportant just the day
I haven't been there since

3.
so you are in me with me now
not out there somewhere like a ghost

not appariton and not
séance calling of the dead

for you are in me with me now
anywhere and always

4.
this day a meditation now on
life and death

on life my life and yours and on
our short lives together

and you are in me with me now
alive in my aliveness

on death, your death and mine

and you are in me with me now

and will be in my dying

5.

I took my time in getting here

and glad I did

we've been here for awhile I feel

just took me time to know it

where you are in me with me now

everywhere and always

****

Writing this paper meant revisiting my large collection of what I call "Dara poems" for the first time in many years and reflecting on the patterns of my mourning. I also took out the last photographs we had taken of him, not knowing then that they would be the last, and reflected on how his life and death had so thoroughly informed my life. I have worked hard at being a good father to Naoise, better than I had been to Dara and better than my own father had been to me.

I came into Gestalt therapy training as part of my openness to change. This involved an obligatory two years of regular therapy, which became fourteen in all. I had stayed in therapy with my female therapist until I felt I had worked with all of the issues I needed awareness about in order to change into always being in becoming me.

Death was a major and recurring theme of my therapy. Dara's death, of course, and my journey through mourning him. And other deaths: all my life I had lived in the shadow of my dead uncle, who had died at the age of fifteen before I was born – and whose name was Seán. I was christened Seán Joseph, always assuming that my second name was after my maternal grandfather. In the late 1990s, my one surviving maternal aunt decided to order a new gravestone for her family grave and to include Dara's name. She also left two spaces blank – one for her and one for me. While checking out of the records, she discovered a grave she knew nothing about – her maternal grandparents – and went to pay her first visit there. She was amazed to see that a four-day old baby was buried there who could not possibly have been her grandparents'. After some further investigation and a conversation with her 95 year-old cousin, she discovered that her mother had given birth to a baby who died in hospital and was secretly buried. It was a boy, and his name was Joseph. So I have been carrying the dead with me all my life. And then my son...

And then another, and wonderful person: in 1988, on a Psychosynthesis residential week in England, I met and fell in love with a younger, beautiful and gentle person, Cathy. I had said something about the congruent wildness of her hair. "It's a wig", she replied and went on to tell me that she had had an operation for a brain tumour and had just completed her course of chemotherapy, so she was actually quite bald. I told her about Dara...and felt a strong urge not to desert her in her illness, to let my love lead me. Less than a year later she moved to Sweden and we lived together until her death in 1993. I took the last six months of her short life off work and was her primary carer up to and including her death. Again, I found myself with a spare bed alongside someone I loved, and this time someone who knew I loved her...and I could hold her hand as she died.

So yes: death and mourning were major themes of my therapy and my Gestalt journey.

No wonder then that I could so easily and honestly respond in the interview:

Belinda: *So the stimulation sustains you?*

Seán: *Yes, always meeting something new, intellectually, socially, meeting different people, new challenges...a phrase that comes to mind right now is 'always being alive'. In some ways I don't have the time to die because I spend so much of my time always being alive.*

Writing this, I am aware more clearly of how inter-connected and integrated the 21 years of my life in Gestalt are with my 22 years of mourning my son and finding meaning. And this is what Gestalt has given me: the opportunity to stay with my grief while recognising my joy, a support for allowing change to happen, a way of being in the world which is also a way of working in and with the world. It means allowing myself to be as gregarious socially as I am, and also still, quiet and reflective in my work as a Gestalt therapist, trainer, supervisor and group facilitator. And no matter how apparently polarised my behaviours may be, I am always me in and through them.

And, right now as I bend over the keyboard, a very special memory: I was working in Belfast in the late 1990s with a supervision group. One of the participants had mentioned her son – Naoise. Another had just become a father to his second son – Dara. So I told them that I felt moved to be reminded of my two sons in the presence of this group.

Previously, when I was asked in purely social settings whether I had any children, I would usually say "Yes, a son". I became accustomed in Gestalt settings to say "Yes, two sons, one living, one dead".

In writing this article, I can feel myself saying "I have two sons, each living though in different ways." And without each and both of them, I would not be who I am today.

So my thanks to my uncles Seán and Joseph, both dead before I was born, and in whose shadow I was raised; to my son Dara who has given so much meaning to my life in his death; to Cathy, who gave life to the word "relationship" in the short time we had together; and to Naoise, my son, companion and best friend in this journey through mourning.

Spirituality and counselling: Not so strange bedfellows

by

Anne Kelliher

I'm really delighted to share with you some reflections on two areas that I find fascinating and am passionate about, i.e., the areas of spirituality and counselling. If counselling is about supporting clients to become their most wholesome selves, then counsellors must be open to working with clients on whatever is of import in their lives as they present in the counselling space. For some, issues of depth, inclusive of their spiritual well-being, is what they may wish to reflect on and work through where necessary. Whilst it is imperative that practitioners should not impose their value system on clients, many authors are encouraging therapists to nourish their own religious and attitudinal systems and to be conscious of the potential value of those of their clients (Hickson & Phelps, 1998). In the words of Colangelo (as cited in Hickson & Phelps) the

> *"process of counselling is strongly a moralistic and value enterprise, as well as a scientific enterprise. Ethics and spirituality are inexorably interwoven into the systematic process of helping clients change".*

It is my hope that the following article will support counsellors and therapists to be more at ease with identifying issues of a spiritual nature, as this area is frequently neglected by training institutions (Ingersoll, 1994; Kelliher, 2007, 2008).

Spirituality, what is it?

On one level, because of its deeply personal nature, one's spirituality is as unique as the individual who holds it. Yet, no matter how one conceptualises one's spirituality, psychologists of religion suggest that there are certain elements, or dimensions, integral to a wholesome spirituality. I will now make some brief comments in relation to the model approach, paying specific attention to the model approaches of Elkins and his colleagues (1988), and Ingersoll (1994).

According to Sperry (2001a), models are simplified representations of reality. They allow for specification of relationships "among ordered observations (taxonomies) of ideas, concepts, or methods......The value and viability of a model is determined by the extent to which it represents the relationship among taxonomies" (Sperry, p.21). The model approaches of Elkins and his team (1988) and Ingersoll (1994) are attempts to create a fuller picture of the essential elements of a wholesome spirituality, based on research. Many similar elements are found in both approaches. Some dimensions are found in one model only. This underlines the limitation of each particular approach and the difficulty in creating an inclusive model of spirituality. I believe the limitations of these model approaches are offset by their strengths.

Background to Elkins' (1988) Model:

Elkins and his team (Elkins et al., 1988) researched spirituality from a humanistic and phenomenological perspective. They embarked on a major literature review of authors who took a phenomenological approach towards spirituality. The end result was a heightened awareness that "spirituality could not be defined simply and that it was a complex, multidimensional construct composed of several major factors" (Elkins et al., p.9). They concluded that "churches and temples do not have a monopoly on spirituality or on the values that compose it. These belong to humanity and are not the exclusive possession of organized religion or of traditionally religious persons" (Elkins et al., p.6).

Elkins et al. (1988) suggested that spirituality is a multidimensional construct with nine major components:- Transcendent dimension, meaning and purpose in life, mission in life, material values, idealism, altruism, awareness of the tragic, sacredness of life, and fruits of spirituality. West (1998a) saw this list as "a fairly comprehensive list of some of the likely topics that can arise around spirituality within the therapeutic relationship" (p.1). Irish based research (Kelliher, 2007) reported a similar conclusion.

Background to Ingersoll's Model:

Ingersoll's (1994) interest in spirituality arose from his practice as a therapist. He was aware of a two pronged approach to spirituality in therapeutic literature. One

144

approach, he felt, was to slight it. In the other, spirituality was viewed as a vital aspect of the client-counsellor relationship and of human development. Ingersoll noted that the latter approach had led to a growing amount of research in the social sciences in the past two decades. One resulting effect was the inclusion of spiritual well-being in the social indicators movement. However, the lack of including "instruction on working with clients in areas of spirituality" (Ingersoll, p.98) in counselling training courses was a concern to him. Ingersoll decided to do a review of the social sciences' literature on spirituality with the following in mind: (a) to create a model of spirituality for counsellors to use in their work with clients, (b) to present spirituality as a construct distinct from religion.

Ingersoll's (1994) review of the research material led him to the following conclusion, that "spirituality like many constructs must be understood as having observable and non-observable elements." (p.100). The observable elements point to a truth that is ever unfolding. In order to avoid the illusion of full explication, Ingersoll used the term *description* instead of definition when speaking of spirituality. He named the following seven components when describing spirituality: meaning, conception of divinity, relationship, mystery, experience, play and integrative dimension (p.101).

The components will now be reflected on in more detail, as they are concrete ways for guiding one in client work where spirituality becomes a factor. By means of this framework therapists can concretely check if a client's spiritual journeying is moving towards a fostering and concretising of the dimensions, or is it a means used by the client to remain infantile, irresponsible, isolated, apart from everyday reality, i.e., less human.

An examination of the components of both models: This section will explore the elements of both models. The elements that are similar to both will be examined first. Relevant insights from spiritual practitioners over the centuries will be noted, as will information from other psychologists of religion. The components of each model can be seen in Table 1:1. I have placed the constructs in each model which speak to a similar dimension of spirituality, as I understand it, side by side.

Table 1.1: Components of the dimensional model of spirituality as understood by Elkins et al. (1988) and Ingersoll (1994)

Elkins et al.	Ingersoll
Transcendent dimension	Conception of divinity
	Mystery
Sacredness of life	
Meaning and purpose	Meaning
Altruism	Relationship
Idealism	
Awareness of the tragic	
Mission in life	
Material values	
	Play
	Experience
Fruit of spirituality	Dimensional integration

The dimensions explored

Transcendent dimension: According to Elkins and his team (1988), the transcendent dimension, seen as "crucial" by West (1998), proclaims that spiritual persons have a sense of the 'more' to life. They are convinced that what is seen is not the whole of reality. This belief, Elkins and his team suggested, is usually grounded on a personal experience of the transcendent, often through what Maslow (1970) termed "peak experiences". They underlined how some people hold a deeply personal relationship with what they have experienced and call it by names such as 'Higher Power', 'God', 'The Divine'.

Others, they said, take a more psychological view believing that this dimension "is simply a natural extension of the conscious self into the regions of the unconscious or Greater Self" (p.10). But whatever the metaphors or typology used to describe this transcendent dimension declared Elkins et al., spiritual individuals believe that "harmonious contact with, and adjustment to, this unseen dimension is beneficial" (p.10). Prayer and commitment to a religion is the end result for many (Hardy, 1980; Worsley, 2000).

The giftedness of an experience of the transcendent was also underlined by Hardy, who noted its availability to those seen by many as unimportant or no friends of the Divine, i.e. "children, atheists and agnostics" (p.2). He strongly advocated the need for psychologists and biologists to explain the religious/spiritual feelings that people experience. He made this call whilst also noting that "science itself can never deal with the real essence of religion any more than it can with the nature of art or the poetry of human love" (p.4).

In naming a transcendent dimension as central to an understanding of spirituality, Elkins and his team (1988) were naming what experts in the field understand to be the core element of every spiritual experience. Hill et al (2000) were explicit in this regard stating:

> The term "spiritual" is used in modern parlance often as a substitute for words like "fulfilling," "moving," "important," or worthwhile." However, ideologies, activities, and lifestyles are not spiritual (even though they can be fulfilling, moving, important, or worthwhile), we would argue, unless they involve considerations of the sacred. The Sacred is a person, an object, a principle, or a

concept that transcends the self. Though the Sacred may be found within the self, it has perceived value independent of the self. Perceptions of the Sacred invoke feelings of respect, reverence, devotion and may, ideally, serve an integrative function in human personality. (p. 64).

The danger of losing sight of this core element and thus reducing spirituality to a fuzzy, no boundaried concept, is a constant challenge. Moberg (2002) pointed out the inescapability of reductionism in all research on spirituality as, "The subject is so ineffable that studying it tends to lower sublime realities to mundane levels, and to translate whatever is inexpressibly sacred into temporal secular concepts." (p. 54). He highlighted how research on spirituality, as with any multidimensional phenomenon, will, at best, only use a few observable data to approximate the phenomenon, and "that always occurs within definitional norms and methodological confines." (p.54).

I now turn to Ingersoll's (1994) understanding of transcendence as contained in the dimensions: conception of divinity and mystery.

Conception of Divinity: Ingersoll (1994) acknowledged that individuals' conception of divinity "may be as diverse as individuals themselves" (p.101). He emphasized that one's conception of divinity has profound implications for how one relates with that divinity and with other human beings. The relationship is also impacted on by one's gender, temperament, demeanour, age, education, colour and culture, he declared. Ingersoll's clarity in naming the subtle and often unnoticed ways one's conception of divinity impacts on, and interplays with, other factors in one's life, was both creative and essential. His appreciation of 'mystery' further highlighted this transcendent element.

Mystery: Ingersoll (1994) emphasised the necessity for a tolerance of mystery, for the "ambiguity of the spiritual" (p.102). Simultaneously, he accentuated the importance and necessity, obligation even, for researchers and spiritual leaders to create some vocabulary that both recognizes the mysterious and provides people with a way to talk about it. He respected the innate difficulty there is in verbalising this element of the spiritual.

Ingersoll (1994) suggested that one way of facilitating the verbalising of mystery is to define the manner in which individuals experience it. He believed that the term 'negative capability' most aptly defined this experience, an experience demanding "the ability to be in mystery or doubt without any irritable reaching after fact or reason" (Keats, as cited in Ingersoll). Negative capability allows a search for meaning which reverences the richness of experience and wherein the lust for certitude is suspended.

It is "the creative moment between old and new meaning. It resembles the phenomenological bracket which wants to 'hold interpretation' so that 'things' can appear in fresh ways" (Shea, 1978, p.46). Western culture with its emphasis on activity, productivity and scientific facts has lowered our tolerance for mystery and interfered with the cultivation and nourishment of the holding of mystery, of tolerating negative capability. Negative capability requires cessation of activity and tolerance of ambiguity, (Smith, 1991). The cessation of activity requires much discipline as it is above all a focus of mind and heart, which in the early stages requires outward cessation of business. It is one of the ingredients on the road to contemplation (Johnston's, 1996).

O' Donohue (1997) suggested that the stories, poetry and prayer of the Celts, used language that is pre-discursive, is permeated by lyrical and reverential observation and is welcoming of mystery. Certainly, his own use of language is full of the mystery of negative capability. For example, "Celtic mysticism recognizes that rather than trying to expose the soul or offer it our fragile care, we should let the soul find us and care for us."(O'Donohue, p.111).

Clients need to be well grounded, with a healthy level of psychological, emotional and spiritual maturity, if they are to navigate safely the realms of negative capability, of "a transpersonal" experience (Sutherland, 2001), an experience of the numinous (Otto, 1978). Sutherland stated it thus:

> *In healthy mental and religious functioning, the line of demarcation separating the two spheres of the personal/ psychological and the transpersonal/spiritual allows for a process of oscillation. ....Oscillation is, for most people, an unconscious process. ......People with high schizotopy are vulnerable to unmanaged oscillation ......(this indicates) a movement into the*

transpersonal that may quickly deteriorate into psychosis.........the profiling of schizotopy identifies people who are not sufficiently integrated, psychologically or spiritually to manage the elements of their exposure to the transpersonal. Open awareness degenerates into boundarilessness." (Sutherland, p.383).

The element of mystery demands psychological and spiritual adulthood, if it is to be negotiated in a wholesome manner. Ekins et al (1988) did not speak of mystery, but their emphasis on the sacredness of life holds some similarities to the dimension of mystery.

Sacredness of life: According to Elkins and his team (1988), spiritual people see life as a whole, as a unity. For them, life is infused with sacredness. They often experience a sense of wonder, reverence and awe even in non-religious settings. They do not "dichotomize life into sacred and secular, holy and profane" (Elkins et al., p.11). Rather, they hold that all of life is holy and that the sacred is in the ordinary, "The spiritual person is able to 'sacralize' or 'religionize' all of life" (Elkins et.al., p.11). According to Dorr (2000b), an Irish theologian, it is only when a person approaches life in this manner that the true sacredness of religious ritual can be experienced in its fullness. In other words, a deep spiritual life is necessary for religious ritual to have personal meaning. The question of meaning is addressed by both models.

Meaning and purpose in life: Elkins and his team (1988) noted that the hunger for meaning and purpose in life is a constant refrain and yearning in humankind. For example, it is repeatedly addressed in psychological (Park, 2005; Frankl, 1946), religious (Macquarrie, 1966; Shea, 2005) and secular (Padovano, 1966) writings. In the view of Elkins et al (1988), the spiritual person has struggled with life's fundamental questions of good and evil, meaning and non-meaning, redemption and loss, and has emerged from the "existential vacuum"(p.11) believing that life in general is deeply meaningful. Elkins and his team accepted that, "The actual ground and content of this meaning vary from person to person" (p.11), but all hold the general tenet that one's own personal life has purpose and meaning. Meaning as understood by Ingersoll (1994) will now be examined.

Meaning : Ingersoll (1994) accepted that whilst meaning is impossible to define in a general way, there are some meaningful moments and general approaches to life which are pointers to what people experience as living meaningfully. He drew on Frankl (1946) to outline what he meant by meaning, i.e. that which the individual experiences as making life worth living. The questions of value, choice and inner freedom to choose one's stance hover in the shadows of this dimension. For many people these choices are overwhelming and some seek counselling support to deal with them (Sperry 2001b).

Ingersoll (1994) believed that humans have an innate will to meaning and that this manifests itself in an individual's searching for the ultimate meaning of his/her life. He viewed the person as body, mind and spirit; spirit being the key. He did not define what he meant by spirit. He held that growth in one's spiritual life, if solid and real, will eventually be manifested in outer behaviour, in one's relationships. Relationships are important aspects of both models.

Relationship: Ingersoll (1994) stressed that the aims of all mythologies, including religious based mythologies, is to address relationships. He suggested that Burns (as cited in Ingersoll) added to the appreciation of the relationship dimension in spirituality by "defining it as a striving for and infusion with the reality of the inter-connectedness among the self, other people and the Infinite/Divine" (Ingersoll, p.102). This is the position held by many in the field of spirituality. Sheldrake (1992) postulated that spirituality's main function is not concern with defining perfection but "with surveying the complex mystery of human growth in the context of a living relationship with the Absolute" (p.50).

Ingersoll (1994) did not spell out what kind of behaviour is indicative of, or integral to, the relationship aspect of spirituality. Elkins et al. (1988) were much more forthcoming in this regard. They spoke of the relationship aspect of spirituality under the headings altruism, idealism and awareness of the tragic.

Altruism: According to Elkins and his team (1988), the inter-connectedness of all humans and a strong sense of lived social justice are integral to the spiritual person. They held that the spiritual person is touched by the suffering and pain of others, and knows that "we are our brother's [sister's] keeper" (p.11). The awareness that "we are all part of the continent of common humanity" (p.11) drives the person to altruistic action, suggested Elkins et al. Altruistic action is a growing theme in spiritual literature (Baum, 2000; Dorr, 2000a, 2000b). Baum and Dorr fleshed out the link between spirituality, social justice and altruism. Altruism shows spirituality to be realistic as well as idealistic. Idealism is another dimension of the model proposed by Elkins et al.

Idealism: According to Elkins and his team (1988), the spiritual person is a visionary and is committed to the betterment of the world. S/he is committed to the actualisation of positive potential in all aspects of life and to high ideals. S/he sees and loves how things/people are whilst also being open to what they may become.

In naming idealism as a component of spirituality Elkins et al. (1988) are in tune with spiritual writers and practitioners, past and present. To accept things and people as they are requires true compassion. Without it, growth cannot happen in a wholesome way, if at all. The writings of Pema Chodron (1994), an American Buddhist nun, captured this compassion clearly. Equally, she enunciated the truth that compassion must first be for oneself. :

Start where you are. This is very important. Tonglen practice (and all meditation practice) is not about luter, when you get it all together and you're this person you really respect. ... You might be the most depressed person in the world ......You might think that there are no others on the planet who hate themselves as much as you do. All of that is a good place to start. Just where you are – that's the place to start. (p.34).

Without such an attitude of compassion towards oneself, one cannot truly embrace another aspect of Elkins et al.'s model of spirituality which is linked to relationship, i.e., awareness of the tragic.

Awareness of the tragic: According to Elkins and his team (1988), a solemn consciousness of the tragic realities of human existence is alive in the spiritual person. Whilst this awareness brings depth and seriousness to him/her, it does not, however, lessen the person's appreciation, joy and valuing of life. The ability to hold such paradoxes and to remain committed to life is, I suggest, linked with the ability to hold mystery and negative capability. Julian of Norwich (Reynolds, 1985)), is a clear example of such a human being. In the midst of tragedy (The Black Plague of the Middle Ages) she held a core belief that "all will be well and all will be well and all manner of things will be well". (Revelations of Divine Love, as cited in Llewelyn, 1985).

This certainty allowed her to meet the day filled with active compassion for her fellow human beings who experienced her as a woman of "goodness, vibrant with faith, hope and love" (Reynolds, p.13). Julian made abundantly clear that the source of her cheerfulness, optimism and serenity rested on her experience of the Transcendent (Revelations of Divine Love, as cited in Llewelyn). The struggle with the tragic continues today and is as real as it was in Julian's day, though the forms of the tragic may be different. According to Elkins et al. (1988), for the spiritual person, awareness of the tragic and of one's relationship with all of creation, gives one a mission in life.

Mission in life: In naming a dimension of their model of spirituality as "mission in life" Elkins and his team (1988) used very traditional religious language. In fleshing out the details of this dimension, they continued in the same vein. The spiritual person, they argued, has "a sense of 'vocation'........a calling to answer.......a destiny to fulfil.....is metamotivated and understands that it is in 'losing one's life' that 'one finds it'" (p.11).

This call is experienced as a sense of responsibility to life. Mission in life is closely allied to another component of Elkins et al.'s model which they named 'material values'.

Material Values: According to Elkins et al. (1988) the spiritual person does not seek ultimate satisfaction in money and possessions. Neither does s/he seek to "use them as a substitute for frustrated spiritual needs."(Elkins et al., p.11), knowing that "ontological thirst" (p.11) can only be satisfied ultimately by spiritual values/gifts. Other authors came to a similar conclusion. Unless human beings recognise their spiritual core, Singer (1990) declared, they will relate to the natural world in a manner that will trap them in a world of material forces, a world resistant to their aspirations of freedom. Buber (1973) believed that people's enslavement to material values resulted in a silencing of the spirit, a cutting off of the spirit from itself.

To have the ability to relate in a wholesome manner with material things, is a hard won stance as recognised by Assagioli (1975), the founder of psychosynthesis:

...spiritual development is a long and arduous journey, an adventure through strange lands full of surprises, difficulties and even dangers. It involves a drastic 'transmutation' of the 'normal' elements of the personality, the awakening of potentialities hitherto dormant, a raising of consciousness to new realms, and functioning along a new inner dimension (p.39).

A similar message was voiced by Ferrucci (1986) who said that "the ultimate choice of whether we want to actualise or betray our potentialities lies within us with all its questions, all its risks, all its beauty and mystery" (p.161). Adults who wish to live in the above manner are known to have sought support in the counselling space (Kelliher, 2007).

Adults who actualise their potential in some meaningful measure have more of a possibility of engaging in play as understood by Ingersoll (1994).

Play: When play is truly playful, individuals forget themselves and give themselves to something greater than themselves, in a giving that is simultaneously pleasurable, according to Ingersoll (1994). This dimension includes all arenas of play. Ingersoll vehemently opposed play for a purpose "such as winning a game or using one's sexuality to control" (p.103). Such caricatures of real play he dismissed as "simply more purposeful work that exacerbates the very things play would refresh." (p.103). He held that it is important to include play as a dimension of spirituality if western seriousness is to be balanced with sincerity. Play, he believed, contains great potential for healing. The playful person is "easy-going, laughter- loving, merry, care-free, and frivolous" (Ingersoll, p.103).

Fox (1991) developed this theme further and suggested that if a person is without an appreciation of play, there is a danger that spirituality may become work or another duty that must be attended to. O'Donohue (1997) was of the same mind when he outlined the consequences of an excessive work ethic. "An excessive concentration on our work, achievements, or spiritual quest can actually lead us away from the presence of love. In the work of soul, our false urgency can utterly mislead us" (p.32). In order to be open to play one must be open to "experience", another dimension named clearly by Ingersoll (1994).

Experience: The spiritual person lives moment by moment, fully present to the ordinary. Ingersoll (1994) stated that "An adequate description of spirituality must refer not only to peak experiences, but also to the ordinary behavioral correlates"(p.103). He emphasized that the sacred aspects of the ordinary are constantly highlighted in Anglican and Catholic sacramental life, in the Islamic Salah and in Zen Buddhism. He suggested that the prescribed ritualistic behaviours in organised religions of all cultures and denominations are "usually ... aimed at cultivating these experiences" (p.104). To live in this manner, open to the sacredness of each moment, one must be in one's own skin, one's own body. The spiritual person is a body person.

Ingersoll (1994) suggested that often when people are talking about looking for meaning in life, what they are really wanting is a vibrant experience of life, of being fully alive, of being fully in their body. This is a recurring theme in spiritual writings over the ages. Underhill (1937), captured this truth vividly. She held that without a sound spiritual foundation one's life is empty, and that "The practical life of a vast number of people is not, as a matter of fact, worth while at all. It is like an impressive fur coat with no one inside it. One sees many of these

coats occupying positions of great responsibility." (p. 33).
In modern parlance the emptiness, isolation and
loneliness of life lived in this manner is poignantly
underscored by the American singer, K.D.Lang (1992), in
her song titled, *"Outside Myself"*:

> *The thin ice covers my soul*
>
> *My body's frozen and my heart*
>
> *is cold and still.*
>
> *...............*
>
> *I've been outside myself for so long*
>
> *Any feeling I had is close to gone*
>
> *I've been outside myself for so long.*

The dis-ease with oneself, with life, portrayed so vividly
in this song is, unfortunately, not uncommon, and
certainly individuals present in the counselling space
grappling with this issue. Such dis-ease, Moore (1992)
held, is the consequence of living out of tune with one's
humanity, one's spiritual longings. Huxley (1977) stated
this truth in other terms. He considered people's need to
transcend self-conscious selfhood as the "principal
appetite of the soul" (p.54). If it is denied, then people

turn to other substances such as drugs and alcohol, which Huxley termed "religion's chemical surrogates" (p.54). Rossetti (1996) approached this numbing of life from a more theological stance. He wrote:

> *"the real danger in failing to live in theos is not depression or burnout but spiritual apathy. ... we may lack interest in anything. We may become people without passion. And when the fire of the 'Spirit' goes out we merely exist. We shuffle along going through the motions and our lives become empty. A spiritual stupor like the mental stupor of asphyxia can result when we do not breathe enough spiritual life." (p.7).*

Rossetti's (1996) statement underlines that the fostering of a spiritual stance within oneself and towards life requires choice, determination, commitment and integration. The 'holding' of life as one, as integrated, was Ingersoll's (1994) final dimension.

Dimensional Integration: Ingersoll (1994) stressed that the dimensions "function as an integrated, synergistic entity", being "complementary, not exclusive categories" (p.104). Spirituality, he said "can be described as synergistically utilising all of the seven dimensions" (p.104). It is, he concluded, "an organismic construct distinct from religion" (p.99). He believed that his approach formed "a new conceptualisation of spirituality and its place in human development and the therapeutic encounter" (p.99).

In underlining the integrative dimension of spirituality, Ingersoll (1994) was in keeping with spiritual thinkers old and new. Spirituality "seeks an integration of all aspects of human life and experience" (Sheldrake, 1992, p.50). It is pervasive of all of life (Moberg, 2001, 2002), and deepens as the person develops psychologically, emotionally, intellectually and socially (Fowler, 1981; Shea, 2005). Such growth demands faithfulness and disciplined co-operation from each individual (Bryant, 1999). Unlike Ingersoll (1994), Elkins and his team (1988) did not speak about integration in the spiritual life. However, it is implicit in their understanding of the fruits of spirituality, the final element they mention as a dimension of their model.

Fruits of spirituality: According to Elkins at al. (1988), if one lives life as outlined in their model, one is incarnating the fruits of spirituality. All dimensions of one's life are permeated by this spirituality. "True spirituality has a discernible effect upon one's relationships, self, others, nature, life, and whatever one considers to be the ultimate." (Elkins et al., p.12).

The constant choice to move either in the direction of spiritual integration/fruits of the spirit or to suppress the sublime, was noted by Grof and Grof (1989). The concept of "repression of the sublime" was coined by Haronian (1972), and refers to the living out of the capacity one has to actively deny or defy the spiritual tendency inside oneself. At the opposite end of this spectrum is spiritual preoccupation. At this point, for whatever reason, one is overwhelmed by spirituality to the detriment of the other dimensions of wellness – emotional, intellectual, social, physical and occupational. Chandler, Holden and Kolander (1992) suggested that spiritual wellness is conceptualised as "at or near the midpoint of this continuum" (p.170), i.e., between repression of the sublime and spiritual emergency/spiritual preoccupation. The need to get support in keeping this balance is of the utmost importance. Chandler, Holden and Kolander (1992) named counselling as a valid means towards fostering a balanced life inclusive of spiritual integration, noting that "assessment and intervention" (p.172) are of the utmost importance.

Challenges to, and guidelines for, spiritual growth

Neither Ingersoll (1994) nor Elkins and his team (1988) gave sufficient guidelines as to how spiritual integration might be accomplished. A knowledge of such supports, especially those that fit readily with the therapeutic process, is imperative for therapists who want to allow clients to look at that dimension of their lives, if clients so wish. This paper does not allow for an in-depth examination of same, but I can point out some appropriate reading, e.g., Assagioli (1986), Boorstein (1980), Burke & Miranti (1995; 2000), Carey (2003), Cashwell & Young, (2005), Cashwell, Myers & Schurts (2004), Cashwell, Young, Cashwell, & Belaire (2001), Chandler, Holden, & Kolander, (1992), Goldberg (1983), Vaughan (1979; 1986), and Walsh and Vaughan (1980).

These practitioners believed that the counselling space is an opportune one in which to reflect on, examine and learn techniques to foster one's spiritual life. Thorne

(1991; 1998), West (2000; 2002) and Thoresen (2000) were of similar mind. .

Conclusion

Spiritually is a lifelong choice. It is a process which can be conceptualised on a continuum. It moves individuals towards a way of life that is inclusive, expanding, and socially aware. Those moving towards spiritual well-being can deal with ambiguity and have a capacity to love that allows the paradoxical combination of gracious acceptance of what is, whilst being motivated to bring about change that results in the greater good. Spiritually driven individuals have deep insight, and a comprehensive and constructive sense of ethics and values. As they grow in maturity, they think globally, but not to the detriment of their immediate situation. Spiritual persons are aware of the need for inner nourishment. For many, this is done with like-minded people who may be drawn from different cultures and faith traditions. A spiritual life can occur within or outside the context of an institutionally organised religion, and not all aspects of religion are assumed to be spiritual.

At the core of one's spiritual life is the awareness of the 'More"' of the 'Transcendent'. It is this awareness that colours and permeates all of the person's life, as it moves from an emphasis on wanting (to have), grasping (to need) and action (to do), to being (to be). Counselling is understood by a growing number of practitioners and researchers as a valid space for clients to reflect on this aspect of their lives.

Bibliography

Assagioli, R. (1975). Psychosynthesis. Wellingborough: Turnstone Press Limited.

Baum, G. (2000). Management in God. The Furrow, 51(5), 267 – 278.

Boorstein, S. (1980). Transpersonal psychotherapy. Palo Alto: Scienceand Behavior Books, Inc.

Bryant, K. (1999). Spirituality for the future. Human Development, 20(2),

Buber, M. (1973). Meetings. Ilinois: Open Court Publishing Company.

Burke, M. T., & Miranti J.G. (Eds.). (1995). Counseling: The spiritual dimension. Alexandria, VA.: American Counselling Association.

Burke, M. T., & Miranti, J. (2000). The spiritual and religious dimensions of counselling. In A handbook of counselling.(pp.601 – 612. Alexandria, VA: ACA Press.

Carey, A. L. (2003). A case for spirituality: Beyond the human level, In The Journal of the Pennsylvania Counselling Association, 5(2), 3-5.

Cashwell, C. S., & Young, J. S. (2005a). Integrating spirituality and religion into Counselling: An introduction. In C. S. Cashwell & J. S. Young (Eds), Integrating spirituality and religion into counselling: A guide to competent practice (pp.1 – 10). Alexandria, VA.: American Counseling Association.

Cashwell, C. S., Myers, J. E., & Schurts, W. M. (2004). Using the Developmental counseling and therapy model to work with a client in spiritual bypass: Some preliminary considerations. Journal of Counseling and Development, 82(4), 403 - 409.

Cashwell, C. S., Young, J. S., Cashwell, T. H., & Belaire, C. (2001). The inclusion of spiritual process in counseling and perceived counselor effectiveness. Counseling and Values, 45(2), 145-153.

Chandler, C.K., Holden, J.M.& Kolander, C.A. (1992). Counselling for spiritual wellness:Theory and practise. Journal of Counselling & Development, 71(2), 168-176.

Chodron, P. (1994). Start where you are: A guide to compassionat living. Boston: Shambhala Publications.

Dorr, D. (2000a). Spirituality and business. The Furrow, 51(7/8), 421 –428.

Dorr, D. (2000b). Sexual abuse and spiritual abuse. The Furrow, 51(10), p.523 – 531.

Elkins, D.N., Hedstorm, L.J., Hughes, L.L., Leaf, J.A. & Saunders, C. (1988). Towards a humanistic-phenomenological spirituality. Journal of Humanistic Psychology, 29(4), 5-18.

Ferrucci, P. (1986) What we may be: The visions and techniques of psychosynthesis. Wellingborough: Turnstone.

Fowler, J. W. (1981). Stages of faith: The psychology of human development and the quest for meaning. San Francisco: Harper.

Fox, M. (1991). Living in an ecological era. Sermon given at St. John's Episcopal Church, Shaker Heights, OH.

Frankl, V.E. (1946). Man's search for meaning. New York: Beacon Press.

Goldberg, P. (1983). The intuitive edge. Wellingborough: Turnstone.

Grof, S. & Grof, C. (1989). Spiritual emergency: When personal transformation becomes a crisis. Los Angeles: Jeremy P. Tarcher.

Hardy, Sir. A. (1980). The spiritual nature of man: A study of contemporary religious experience. Oxford : Clarendon Press.

Haronian, F. (1972). Repression of the sublime. New York: Psychosynthesis Research Foundation.

Helminiak, D. (1987). Spiritual development: An interdisciplinary study. Chicago: Loyola University Press.

Hickson, J., & Phelps, A. (1998). Women's spirituality: A proposed practice model. In D. S. Becvar (Ed.), The family, spirituality and social work, pp.43 – 57. The Hawthorn Press, Inc.

Hill, P. C., Pargament, K.I., Hood, Jr., R.W., Mccullough, M.E., Swyers, J.P., Larson, D.B., & Zinnbauer, B.J. (2000). Conceptualizing religion and spirituality:Points of commonality, points of departure. Journal for the Theory of Social Behaviour, 30(1), 51 –77.

Ingersoll, R.E. (1994). Spirituality, religion and counselling: Dimension and relationships. Counselling and Values, 38, 98-111.

Johnston, W. (ed.). (1996). The cloud of unknowing and the book of privy counselling. London: Fount Paperbacks.

Kelliher, A. T. (2007). An exploration of spirituality, faith & religion in the counselling context. Unpublished Ph. D. thesis

Kelliher, A. T. (20. 06. 2008). The model approach to spirituality: It's implications for counselling practice.

Lecture given at The joint conference of the division of counselling psychology of Ireland and Britain , 20,21 June, Trinity College Dublin, 2008.

Lang, K.D. (1992). Outside myself. Ingenue. New York: Sire Records Company.

Llewelyn, R. (Ed.). (1985). Julian: Woman of our day. Darton, Longman & Todd: London.
Macquarrie, J. (1966). Principles of christian theology. London: SCM Press Limited.

Maslow, A.H. (1970). Religion, values, and peak experiences. New York: Viking.

Moberg, D.O. (2002). Assessing and measuring spirituality: Confronting dilemmas of universal and particular evaluative criteria. Journal of Adult Development, 9(1), 47 –60.

Moore, T. (1992). Care of the soul: How to add depth and meaning toyour everyday life. London: Piatkus.

O'Donohue, J. (1997). Anam chara: Spiritual wisdom from the celtic world. London: Bantam Press.

O'Donohue, J. (1998). Eternal echoes: Exploring our hunger to belong. London: Bantam Press.

Otto, R. (1978). The idea of the holy London: Oxford University Press.

Park, C. L. (2005). Religion and meaning. In R. F. Paloutzian & C. L. Park (Eds.), Handbook of the psychology of religion and spirituality, (pp.295 – 314). New York: The Guildford Press.

Padovano, A. T. (1966). The estranged God. Sheed & Ward: New York

Reynolds, A. M. (1985). Woman of hope. In R. Llewelyn, (Ed.), Julian: Woman of our day. London: Darton, Longman and Todd.

Rossetti, S.J. (1996). Spiritual asphyxiation. Human Development, 17(4), 5 – 10.

Shea, J.J. (1978). Stories of God. Chicago: Thomas Moore Press.

Shea, J.J. (2005). Finding God again: Spirituality for adults. New York: Rowman & Littlefield Publishers, Inc.

Sheldrake, P. (1992). Spirituality and history: Questions of interpretation and method. New York: Crossroad.

Singer, J. (1990). Seeing through the visible world. San Francisco: Harper and Row.

Smith, M.L. (1991). A season for the spirit. Cambridge: Crowley

Sperry, L. (2001a) Approaches to transformation. Human Development,22(1), 16 – 21.

Sperry, L. (2001b). Spirituality in clinical practice. Philadelphia:Brunner-Routledge.

Sutherland, M. (2001). Developing a transpersonal approach to pastoral counselling. British Journal of Guidance and Counselling, 29(4), p.381 – 390.

Thoresen, C. E. (2002). Unpublished lecture. Guest Lecturer, NUI.,Cork.

Thorne, B. (1991). Person-centred counselling : Therapeutic and spiritual dimensions. London : Whurr Publications.

Thorne, B. (1998). Person-centred counselling and christian spirituality.London: Whurr Publishers.

Underhill, E. (1976). The spiritual life. Homebush, N.S.W.: Society of St. Paul.

Vaughan, F (1979). Awakening intuition. New York: Doubleday.

Vaughan, F. (1986). The inward arc: Healing and wholeness in psychotherapy and spirituality. Boston: Shambhala.

Walsh, R. N. & Vaughan, F. (1980). Beyond ego: Transpersonal dimensions in psychology. Los Angeles: Tarcher.

West, W. (1998, March). The spiritual space in the counselling relationship. Paper presented at the Durham Conference, Durham.

Worsley, R. (2000). Can we talk about the spirituality of counselling? Counselling, 12(2), 89 - 91.

Inviting the Angel

Counselling and Therapy as Sacred Work

by

Mark Ryan

I was raised in the Catholic tradition, by two devout, and dogmatic parents. I was schooled in the Catholic tradition, by many devout and dogmatic nuns and priests. I was inspired by several priests, who took the approach that they would rather have a class of questioning atheists than one full of unquestioning believers.

To all of them, I owe a depth of gratitude that I can only repay by "passing it on". I dedicate this article to all of them. I daresay that they would be amazed that what they told me didn't go in one ear and out the other, as I also daresay, they strongly suspected.

My professional origins are as a General and Mental Health Nurse, training in Gestalt Therapy and several hundred ours of Jungian Analysis - the latter two, perhaps an antidote to the former two.

My vocation is currently exercised by my role as a counsellor in a Youth Health Service in Canberra. I work with young people between the ages of twelve, and twenty five. The service is free, and, for the most part, overbooked.

My first memories of Catholicism are from about the age of four, being dragged off to mass, every Sunday, and Holy Day of Obligation, as well as the odd bonus weekday mass at 7 am. The words "Thanks be to God" at the conclusion, were the ones I prayed most fervently, as I thanked God that it was over.

My mother never once said that she wanted me to be a priest, and, never once needed to. I just knew, from an early age, that such was the case. Having disposed of my virginity at the ripe old age of seventeen, I decided that celibacy and I were two mutually exclusive entities.

Nevertheless, the role modelling of Caritas by the Vincentian Fathers, (given their unenviable task of my secondary education), my own father's involvement in the

St Vincent de Paul Society, my mother's devotion to Legionis Mariae were both sufficiently powerful that "a job" was out of the question. Whatever I chose to do with my life, it would have to be a "vocation".

And so, I went nursing. Initially I did general nursing back in the days when nurses trained in hospitals, and then subsequently psychiatric nursing. I shudder to recall the impact of witnessing souls suffering and dying on the extremely sensitive, perceptive and naïve eighteen year old boy from the country I then was. I shudder more so at the impact of being constantly in contact with those in the thrall of madness.

As the health system endured the "death by a thousand cuts" of economic rationalism, I continued to attempt to fulfil my vocation. Along the way, encountering a gestalt therapist or three, whose approach to the mad and the worried well I initially viewed with cynicism and suspicion (being a devotee of the DSM III). However I underwent a gradual, profound and permanent conversion.

This led to gestalt therapy training, in 1990, at the Sydney Gestalt Centre, and, subsequently, in '93 and

'94, through the Illawarra Gestalt centre, where I heard the words "Good Gestalt is though you, not from you!" and that, perhaps, as you worked with your clients, so too did the grace of God.

And so too did it act on my own life.

In October 1992, "the Grace of God got in the way" (to coin a line from a song called "Some People Change", by Montgomery Gentry, an American Country Duo). During the course of a chaotic double shift on an acute psychiatry ward, a client in the thrall of psychosis attempted to strike a colleague, and in the ensuing "restraint", I managed to injure my back - permanently.

A nurse with a buggered back is about as much use as an ashtray on a motorbike.
I was placed on "light duties, clerical", and, as I saw it, my vocation was lost.

As Jung has said, the God's reveal themselves through illness. Not that I could see this at the time, being stuck in grief and despair, doomed, as I saw it to execute meaningless clerical functions.

Somewhere in this time, between injury and light duties, I experienced my first episode of "influx" as Van Dusen describes the profound, mysterious, spontaneous and overpowering flooding of Spirit into one's being. It is impossible to describe in any way which is adequate. "Touched by the finger of God" is the metaphor I used at the time, and it will suffice.

Tears well up, as I recall this.

Somewhere around four in the morning, on night duty, it began. A complete and utter shift of awareness, a breakthrough into a feeling of being everything I possibly could be, of being one hundred percent alive, incandescent, "lit up" by Spirit, and drawn into an awareness of God's Love powering everything in the physical universe, from the nucleus of an atom to the indescribable vastness of galaxies, and all in between. It lasted for fourteen hours. Fourteen hours of the influx of Grace. No sleep, no fatigue, just aliveness, in its full, magnificent intensity. Thankfully, with a friend, an experienced Psych Nurse, who had the charity to listen, and reassure me that I wasn't manic.

A bit less than a year after my injury, again, by the grace of God, I found myself in the sacred space of a Jungian Analyst, Patricia Moroney, to address the depression that the loss of my role and the constant pain had engendered. And, so, to the long, slow, excruciating haul and trawl, dredging the detritus of my wounded-ness (after I type this, I am aware of the Latin noun "crux, cruces", meaning cross).

As I look back on it, it was a process of sacrifice, the process of "making sacred" (as I perceived it) my "ashtray on a motorbike" worthlessness. It was the alchemical process of turning lead into gold with words, sand play, and dreams.

Most profound was one particular dream, experienced whilst Patricia was on sabbatical in Europe.

Within this dream, I saw Patricia, wearing a nun's veil, kneeling down before what I interpreted as a massive headstone, offering something to it. On her return, I reported the dream to her. She became quite perturbed, checked her diary, and informed me that on the night of my dream, she had been praying at a Holy Shrine in Greece. What I discovered later, by sheer happenstance, was that, for most of her adult life, she had been a Dominican nun!

Hmmm, there was certainly more to the therapeutic relationship than what was obvious.

Now we fast forward to 1999, when I had escaped the clutches of light duties, and, to my exceeding gratitude, a return to clinical duties, on a crisis team. I am on a home visit to a suicidal eighteen year old woman with her boyfriend. I was with a Psych Nurse colleague, and dear friend Herb. He was interviewing, I scribing. Her boyfriend reported grinding of teeth, both when asleep, and also, when awake, though she was rarely conscious of it, unless it was reflected to her. It was normal practice to complete the assessment before the actual "intervention".

I became aware, utterly convinced, that if I let this moment pass, it would be forever lost, so I interrupted Herb, and leapt in. A very quick explanation of Reich's body armouring, and a very, very quick summary of relevant gestalt theory ensued, followed by the counselling work. What I will never forget is my own experience of the Work. It was as if I was being "guided", and not only was I absolutely, utterly certain of what I was doing, or, perhaps, better said, what was being done through me, I also "knew" verbatim , what the young woman would say next, for the entire session.

A small part of me was sitting on my shoulder, thinking "Wow, where is this coming from?" The other thing that I recall was a sensation of "energy" emanating from around my sternum, surging out, and into the young woman. I choose to classify it as "Divine Love", of which I was being Graced with being the conduit for. Unsurprisingly, it was a picture perfect vignette of gestalt therapy, and, satisfied those words "through you, not from you".

It ended with the most beautiful act of young woman her face in post cathartic softness, weeping, clutching the pillow of her 8 year old self, rocking gently, and no longer suicidal. When asked what she needed for closure, she requested to be able to hug both Herb and myself. (I am again, close to tears as I recall this experience). The only on going treatment I could suggest was that she procure a copy of "Jonathon Livingstone Seagull and read it. She did not re-present in the ensuing twelve months, unusual to say the least.

For our own closure, we drove around the corner, got out of the car for a smoke, and promptly burst into tears. Herb stated that, in all his years of working in psychiatry, he had never seen anything like this Work.

I don't know what actually happened in that sacred space and that sacred moment, but I choose to believe that an Angel stepped in, perhaps, and gave me the truly humbling experience of how deeply and utterly sacred the work of a therapist is. How honoured, and, how unworthy, and how deeply grateful I feel to this day.

And so now, I find myself, a counsellor - again, by the Grace of God.

After a critical incident happened to me in 2004, including a death threat, and a breakdown (though Patricia, quite rightly, saw it as a breakthrough) I later departed psychiatry, and departed nursing, after twenty five years. It took a great leap of faith to leave the certitude and security of a form of work which had long since been eating away, eroding my soul.

And which I had outgrown (as I look back) many years before.

I interviewed for the position of Counsellor some four years ago. In all my career, it was the first interview I felt that I had done well. It ran for an hour and fifteen minutes. At its conclusion, unlike any other job application, I somehow managed to let go of the outcome, and leave the rest "in God's hands", quite consciously. If I was meant to get the job, I'd get it. And, by the Grace of God, this so very sacred task came my way, served to satisfy my heart and soul need to exercise my vocation.

I now work in an organization which very deliberately and mindfully lives to its Christian values, without any need to jam them down anyone's throat.

And, so often, I recall the experiences which led me here. They remind me, again and again, of how truly sacred the Work is.

Each morning, in preparation for my day, I sit outside with my coffee and cigarette, and pray three rosaries. (That old Catholic tradition again!! In doing so, I pray for all my clients, first and foremost. Then I pray for – guidance, for compassion, for understanding, and, for the right words and actions. I ask to be granted the

Grace of living the Prayer of St Francis - "Make me a channel of Your peace...".

And, so as I don't feel like I am alone in my chair, I invite the Angel to be there with me, beside me, within me.

In the four years I have been employed as counsellor, I have accepted all but two clients, both sexual abuse victims, who were referred on to female specialist counsellors. These were not the only sexual abuse victims, just two that my intuition told me needed a female worker. I have had no need to refer any client to the mental health Crisis Team. (The best way to deal with a crisis is not to provoke one in the first place). Not one client has made a suicide attempt, though many have experienced suicide ideation.

I see my office not as a "clinical" space, but as a "temenos", a sacred space, far more akin to a confessional than a part of a "health service". I see the Work, as an opportunity for Divine Love to manifest itself. Somewhere along the way, I lost the symptom thieving arrogance of psychiatry - again, by the Grace of God.

I see the client, not as a series of problems, to be "fixed", but as someone who carries within them the "imago dei", the image of God. I hope I am able to help them in their "becoming", as we dance, laugh, cry, struggle, challenge, and generally bumble and stumble along to a more authentic way of being-in-the–world.

And, I remember that the "logos" of the "psyche" means not "knowledge" of the brain, or the mind, but an "understanding" of the spirit, the soul or butterfly, as are the literal translations of the word.

And so, the Work is sacred.

So to, the lives it comes in contact with, both the clients', and my own.

Gaudeamus!!

Intimacy and Couples Therapy

By

Esperanza Cardona

This article is divided into three sections. The first section explores the meaning of intimacy, the goal of intimacy and how it can be satisfied in primary couple relationships.

The second section presents issues leading to the breakdown of the capacity to sustain intimacy in couples, and the role of shame as an inhibitor to the restoration of intimacy.

The third section presents a Gestalt therapy model for couples' therapy, based on developing self and partner support for the expression of intimacy.

What is intimacy?

Couple's intimacy is a special kind of contact that requires power balance between partners and nurtures self-discovery and meaning making In doing so, it enables the lifelong journey of individual growth

Additionally, intimacy leads to the creation of a healthy couple's self understood as the shared reality that is unique to the partners and cannot be replicated by any two other individuals.

It is the nature of human beings that we grow into existence from within another. As such our innermost memory of 'being' is that of being one with another. This beginning in connection is followed by a physical separation at birth that sees us living as individuals albeit within our environment, to the end of our days. (Viorst, 1986). It is this original experience of interrelatedness, later on sustained by our living as part of the external field that drives our primal need to seek intimate connection throughout our lives. (Viorst, 1986)

In intimate relationships the type of connection we seek transcends the functional contact whose sole purpose is the satisfaction of a need . What we yearn for is the intimate contact we were born into: the felt experience of interrelatedness whereby we are both one, and one with another, (five states of the soul; man's search for meaning) that satisfies the fullness of our core sense of self. It is this blueprint of the felt sense of self that makes intimacy a lifelong need (Wheeler et al, 1994).

While nurturing relationships with intimate moments can occur in different dyads such as between parent and child, siblings, friends, and therapist and client (reference), an intimate relationship (as opposed to a nurturing relationship with intimate moments) has a unique quality to it: the personal disclosure that occurs is driven by the sole purpose of being known and is not instrumental to any other goal (Wheeler et al, 1994).

This points to the challenge of keeping intimacy in the couple's relationship, as the desire for individual goals which calls for collaboration between partners, coexists with the need to simply be known and needs to be negotiated (a struggle between separateness and togetherness).

In contrast with self-validated disclosure witnessed by the other, self-revelation which carries the need for the other to make ok for us what we ourselves are not ok with, is not couple's intimacy . Though this self-revelation brings with it the possibility of feeling accepted, not shamed, which when accomplished embodies an intimate moment, it has a power imbalance inherent in the need for the other to create our sense of 'being ok' in spite of our experience. In other words, the emotional dependence on the other to introduce into our world the sense of being ok creates a power imbalance incompatible with couples' intimacy (Schnarch, 1994).

Hence, couple's intimacy is born out of self-validated revelation that is witnessed by the other. Intimate witnessing involves an acknowledging response which includes an appreciation of our integrity (reference). It requires power balance at an emotional level which in turn comes from having a largely equal capacity to influence the direction the couple takes in spite of financial or other perceived differences between them.

The goal of intimacy

Intimacy and the goal of intimacy (Wheeler et al, 1994) are two different things. Intimacy is a type of connection that transcends the merely contactful aspect of a relationship which enables need satisfaction. It goes a step further, whereby the need being satisfied is no other than the very act of being accepted in one's own integrity (reference). This is step one. Step two, the goal of intimacy, is enabling the fresh articulation of the individual's subjective field, the lifelong journey of meaning making through contact (Wheeler et al, 1994) which defines the very essence of being human.

Self-validation is essential to intimate couple relationships, as an indicator of power balance. In the ongoing process of meaning-making which is innate to our human nature (Schnarch, 1994, Wheeler et al, 1994), self-validation enables intimacy, by allowing disclosure to be for the purpose of self-discovery in the presence of the other, and for being known by the other.

Intimacy and the couple's self

The impact of intimacy is a capacity to be changed by the experience of the other which leads to the creation of the couple self, a co-created intimate universe unique to the couple and which cannot be replicated by any two other partners. Without this permeability to the other, intimacy stops at a distant appreciation of the integrity of the other, at its best need-satisfying contact.

In intimate relationships the desire for the other comes from the longing to be within that universe (1) that provides us with a warm reception for who we are, (2) where we can continue to feel alive by virtue of the witnessed process of making new meaning for the questions "who am I?" and "what sense do I make of life or this or that event?", and (3) where we can be contributors to its healthiness by engaging on the intimate dialogue that defines the essence of a couple's relationship (reference) in response to our partner's presence in our lives.

Intimacy and sexuality

In couples, intimacy is not just about the individual's experience of being received but also about the couple making new meaning together, both for their individual sense of self and within the co-created couple self, effectively co-creating the world of two as one that gives full expression to the blueprint of intimacy we were born into. In this regard sexuality has the potential to epitomize couple self creation through the actual process of sharing, increasing and celebrating love (Schnarch, 1994).

Sexuality is a powerful dimension in which a couple brings into the foray their innermost fears and desires – a huge potential to grow intimacy and couple self, enabled through the language of sex: the possibility to ask for what's desired, to selflessly give more than wanted for the joy it brings up in the other, to take more than your fair share, to take the risk of being selfish and find oneself welcome. The opportunity to give and take in any measure and then to give and take together, to explore being one together and then two again, the dance of togetherness and individuality and the blissful possibility of feeling accepted in both, confluence and differentiation.

D. Schnarch (1994) in *Psychology Today* pp.38,(10).

T. Moore (1998). *The Soul of Sex*. Harper Collins Publishers, N.Y.

G. Wheeler & S. Backman (1994). *On Intimate Ground*. Jossey-Bass (1994), San Francisco.

J. Melnick & S.M. Nevis (1994). Intimacy and Power in long-term relationships: A Gestalt Therapy-Systems Perspective in *On Intimate Ground*. Jossey-Bass (1994), San Francisco.

Observing Grief

By

Gary Hodson

"Oh what a world we live in
Oh what a world my parents gave me ..."

Rufus

Wainwright

("Want One")

Since the time of my grandmother's death, my first experience of a significant personal loss, back in 1976, I have been drawn by the subject of loss and grief. Other losses since have enabled me to learn more about the impact of loss on myself, studying within the discipline of loss and grief and of counselling has put me in touch with up-to-date research, techniques and ideas for dealing with and counselling for loss and grief.

However it has been in my "hands on work" as a Clergy person, as a Counsellor and often as a friend and confidant that I have actually been able to draw my own life experiences, my education and my work experience into a useful, practical and dare I say often healing tool. When I see 'healing' I don't mean helping people to "get over it", that's impossible. Rather I work with people so that they are enabled to rebuild a different, new life that takes into account the loss they have suffered.

Grief is often a devastating experience, it can tear people apart, and it often tests the strongest, terrifies others and amazingly appears to leave a few unscathed. Grief has became a major subject in its own right academically and in University curriculum since the 1990's, however at this moment I'm intending to leave the theory to another time; it's something of the experience of observing grief that I want to share.

Although I have observed and experienced grief over some 40 years now, the period of the early 1990's until the 2004 were intense, confronting and invaluable for me as a man, as a human being and as especially as a clinician. At that stage little of worth had been written and of what there was Kubler-Ross was far and away the most practically grounded I came across.

In the early 1990's, in my first country parish (as a clergy person) I saw approximately 95 funeral a year, over half of which I was directly responsible for dealing with. At the other end of this time span, I had spent a number of years as a counsellor in a private hospital working mostly in oncology and to an extent with miscarriage, still birth and neo-natal trauma.

On one particular occasion I was brought in just at the end of a heart breaking situation where an adolescent boy had been playing with his mates on the edge of flood waters just near his home. The boy had slipped, fallen in the water and gone under; no-one had seen him since.

After an intensive search of 2 days his grandfather found his body washed up on his own land. When the grandfather found the lad he had a minor heart attack.

The husband, the boys Dad, had been "minding" him, so he blamed himself, the mother also blamed him and herself for being at work, his elder sisters suffered their own loss and saw their parents torn apart.

In preparing the funeral I discovered that this family was part of a much larger close, family network and that they were well loved people in their own small town. The father was one of nine children and virtually all of them and their families still lived nearby. That's how I first met the Grandmother (lets call her Nance).

Several months later I had become intimately involved in supporting the grieving parents, so when the father's brother was found dead in bed (with his child beside his), the family called me and literally said "please help us".

Nance was devastated, this older lady had worked hard to raise nine children, she had loved being a part of the lives of some 23 grandchildren and was a great grandmother, yet she had never suffered loss like this. Then while we were burying her son a police car stopped with the shocking news that one of the daughters (a mother of three) had been killed in an accident on her way to the funeral.

Several weeks later Nance's husband suffered a fatal heart attack.

At the end of 7 months this happy, innocent loving family lost 4 intimate family members and an uncle and aunt. I had the honour, and the horror, of performing the services for all six of them.

I often look back and think "what bloody good did I do for them?"; yet there is also a part of me that knows and even admires what I did. Essentially I didn't aim to "do" anything, other than be there with them, guiding, supporting caring, sharing tears and holding whoever.

In the days, weeks, and then months ahead I built a team of support people and counsellors around the family which proved both necessary and a very wise move for the family as well as for me. However I am now quite convinced that the real work at the time was not an excellent follow up but rather to arrive and say something to the effect of "Oh Nance, I'm speechless, there's nothing to say, can I just come and sit with you?" Nance recalled later that this was the best thing anyone said; even in the event she knew that she did not want platitudes, she didn't even want talk, she needed to be what she was in the moment: a suffering, exhausted, bewildered, hurting old women and mother.

I sat with her in that dreadful, empty feeling and I'm pleased with the option I found to be simply "present" to and for Nance along with many of this extended family.

-

In a different place and at a different time, in quite another context a situation faced me that was more challenging than I had expected to be dealing with.

Having been the father of five children who didn't survive to birth I am keen to assist people facing the loss of their hopes through miscarriage, as well as those scarred by premature births and people facing a still birth. At one stage in my training I had done a one day a week 12 month placement in a neo-natal ward to an extent because of this and my willingness to be involved I was sometimes called on by various hospitals, in the ACT & later in NSW.

To this work I was able to bring my own experiences, the thoughts and comments of people who had "been there" themselves, my academic learning and maybe more valuable than that the wisdom of a women I worked with in Sydney who had made working with still birth her career. It seemed to me that as a man having these four advantages to call upon enabled me to bring something of real value to situations that were often so terribly bleak.

A local family were excited about their daughter coming out of a very difficult relationship, who had then meet another man and was now having a child to him, a sibling to her two children by the previous relationship.

A phone call came from maternity asking that I go to the labour ward as quickly as possible. I arrived to be told that the baby was almost full term, the delivery had not gone well and that the hospital had realised a disaster was probably just around the corner.

And they were correct, it was.

A little girl had been birthed, obvious weak, undersized and not properly formed. The mother was beside herself, knowing how it was "meant to happen" and knowing this felt all wrong. The man, a first time father and in all probability overwhelmed by the medical world in a hospital, was dazed, disorientated and clearly fearful.

The hospital staff were very good to this fairly simple couple, as they were with the baby and they were careful to include me and what I brought to the situation. In that miserable delivery room, there was a sense of respect, shared grief and care. That is a hopeful combination for doing the best that can be in such a trying circumstance; I knew well the difference, not having always worked with such an advantage.

When the baby was cleaned up just a little, and the specialist was still on the way, she was offered to her mother, who was shield away in fear, presumably scared of what she was going to see. At that juncture I took and nursed the baby, sitting beside the Mum, with the Dad on the other side of the bed. From there I describe to them what I could see, carefully highlighting some of the things that normalised their baby. Eventually the babe let out a small whimper and on that note I was able to hand her to her Mother.

The Dad was still horrified, I assumed he had no idea of what to do, but I suspect he really just wanted to run. As the Mother became accustomed to her baby I talked with the Dad over them, getting him to engage with what she was doing and finally suggesting that he hold her hand as she caressed their daughter. Very tentatively he did so. Within moments the Mum was actually nursing the babe to her chest while she and the Dad were crying; so rightfully.

The news when the specialist had examined the baby was as bad as it could be; he gave her only an hour or so to live. So amid tears and fear and requests to call in both of their families we moved this small family to another room and settled in to wait the term of their child's life.

Initially a few family trickled in, then they flooded into the small room and with them tears, sorrow and comfort flowed. In many ways at this point they did their own work of acceptance and grieving. Soon natural events overtook and made the ending of life clear as the baby's life visibly ebbed, until finally she was completely still and there was complete silence in that pressing crowd. Then, as if on a signal accompanied by her last breath, a combined wail of shared grief and horror began.

It was heart wrenching.
It was authentic.
Foreign it was to me; it was good.

After her death we were able to keep the baby with us for quite some time, and gradually I talked with the family drawing them from horror to being able to engage and interact with this life that had been such an important part of us. In my humble opinion this baby was absolutely honoured, loved and accepted as an eternal member of this whole family.

I experienced that as a wonderful thing in the midst of such tragedy.

Over the following days more time was spent with the baby, her parents, her siblings and grandparents. During this process we began to plan a funeral as a farewell and especially as something of a formalised releasing of her to eternity. That was not easy; together we exhausted many boxes of, each and every one of us. Yet a point came where it felt that we were there, what was needed was now planned.

On the day of the funeral I went to the morgue first with the funeral people, then we met the parents who joined the hearse at the hospital; we carried this baby, between us in a basket, then we drove past the home of the family and on to the cemetery. There music was played including a song chosen by her parents "My Little Ray of Sunshine". People spoke of the baby's significance to them, others spoke of their feelings and their sense of her having been among us. Her actual burial was heartbreaking, and yet I sense it also heralded a change in the journey.

I was able to keep in close contact with these people for quite sometime. Retrospectively it was a very hard road for them, with conflict, tears and regret. Yet well down the track I sensed the adults and the children gradually building a life which remembered the place owned by this baby, but also moving them to a new place, a life different from their dreams, but a new life none-the-less.

My constant reflection after work such as this: what did I contribute, how do I feel, about the usefulness of my "work and expertise'? I feel it was valuable, it was worthwhile and I am not sorry that I lived that life, and had the opportunity to be part of such a scene and to be with such a family.

The reality may well be that quite without me they would have managed, yet statistics inform us that a stream of disasters often follow the death of a child, (according to some including a 75% break up of the parental relationship). The death of any child in Western society is usually accompanied by heart break, loneliness, isolation and suicide attempts may follow that. My assessment is that I saw something there in the parents and among this extended family, which was more hopeful than that. If I assisted to nurture a "hopeful" outcome, then I can feel satisfied.

What worked I ask myself yet again?

Well who knows for sure, but I think part of it may have been sharing grief, as was my preparedness to be real, hand in hand with that would be my being prepared to be vulnerable and being a silent, peaceable, gentle presence to these grief stricken people.

I feel sure that at some points my prior experience of death, maternity wards, hospitals and planning "good" funerals was important, however I really think that being present was the key. Present with and for those in need.

J stands for Resilience

by

Sheryl Wiffen

What can I say about a lady who lived on the street at Port Kembla for twelve Years? I mull over words and stare at my scribblings; notes from the glimpses I had of one woman's life. In my contact with J over the past twelve years, I do not presume to have *known* her. However, I am left with visions, snapshots in my mind of an amazing, independent, resilient aboriginal woman. What would she allow me to say if she knew I was to speak *about* her? Probably, "Fuck off! It's none of your business"! J was a private person. To say she didn't trust anyone is an understatement. Life on the street fed mortar into her brick wall against life. I wonder, lady of the gorgeous golden legs, what were your dreams and hopes before life corrupted your thoughts?

I'm aware of my internal discussion and am challenged with a decision: what to do? Should I just hold you in my heart and keep it to myself? I stumble on how to begin and as I write, I have begun! Again, I read the scrappy notes and phone numbers of family; and contact services and various people who were drawn into her dying process, a process I became a part of in May 2007. And, by July, J lay in palliative care at Port Kembla Hospital. A once feisty spirited, proud and defiantly self reliant woman, now a prisoner in her pain wracked body. The best legs on Wentworth Street could no longer stand up.

My first memory of her was late one night around twelve years ago when I was an Outreach Worker with SWOP (Sex Worker Outreach Program). My co-worker, Lizzie and I had been to six parlours providing support and resources, so by the time we reached Wentworth Street we needed coffee. There was no opportunity for coffee out there at 1am. Our usual route was to drive up and down the main drag, around the back via the laneways, and then we would park close to the four corners where the girls stand; we could approach street-working girls while they were not busy.

As we loaded paper bags full of condoms and lube into plastic carry bags, workers approached the car. No relaxed conversation over coffee while tucked into a comfy lounge here! Everyone's working the street, surveying the cars and trucks cruising past, any distraction could cost a job. For many the consequence of this could be painful heroin withdrawal: aluminium taste in the mouth, aching bone marrow, sweating and shaking, vomiting, cramps and sleeplessness. We wandered down the street, stopping at intervals to chat with girls we knew.

About twenty five metres away I saw a golden-brown skinned woman dressed in an Akubra, tasselled white leather jacket with matching knee high, country heeled boots: the Divine Miss J! I thought I'd had a vision. Nobody in Wentworth Street dressed like this. Our introductory line was "Hi we're from SWOP. We bring condoms and info for the Working Girls here".

That was all that we were able to inject into the conversation for around half an hour. This stunning figure standing on the top end of Wentworth Street spewing a tirade of fire and venom, vomiting her injustices, frustration and sense of lost hope. Yelling to us, her audience, about her experiences of being treated deplorably! What I didn't know then was that J's brother had recently died in tragic circumstances, around the time that she had come to Wollongong.

What becomes of a girl-child born in a hospital forty odd years ago? At that time, indigenous people were considered part of the flora and fauna. Aboriginal women were *not* considered legally human!

As J lay helplessly dying in hospital, her Mum shared with me some of the intricacies of her life and experiences. She shared the painful memories of her cries for help in the hospital during her labour pains, only to be refused any comfort or courtesy. She eventually gave birth to her daughter in the toilet! I heard this incredible woman re-visit memories of J's childhood; of the challenges she faced raising three children alone. Of how she had bandaged her own scalded arms in plastic wrap and worked as a cleaner, in order to earn the funds to pay for her skin grafts. She had been severely burnt from head to toe.

The curtains were drawn in J's hospital room because she couldn't stand the light. I watched J's sister stroke her face and massage moisturiser into her scaly, dying skin while chatting to her, rekindling childhood memories. As I listened to them, I learnt that J loved Fleetwood Mac, Cat Stevens and Simon & Garfunkel. A faint glimmer of a smile graced J's lips when we spoke of her brand new grand daughter. Someone had placed a photo of the baby on the bedside table.

Shouldn't the questions be "How long can a woman survive on the streets, homeless in Australia? How does this happen in our *civilised* society? Shouldn't we in our self-centred, consumer orientated, individualistic society care about such people? Why are we so self centred and judgemental? What would it have been like to have walked in her shoes?"

In Port Kembla a culture has developed where the working girls are seen by many of the community as receptacles for all the un-dealt with hatred and fear; and conversely, there is a recognition of them as being practising *therapists* for men seeking their services.

During those twelve years there were many incidents. One such incident saw J receive a blow to the head from someone wielding a house brick. A deep right-angled dent in the top of her head needed stitches, however we were unable to convince her to seek medical attention. At the time she confided in me, that she did not trust the medical profession (one of the miniscule bits she had told me about herself). So, the day J came to the Port Kembla Community Project requesting assistance to get to a hospital because of her intense head pain and dizziness, I was immediately responsive, assuming the pain to be serious. I knew this was a request outside of her normal behaviour.

At the Medical Centre, I was frustrated by the interview with the doctor as J was doubled up in pain beside me. His interest was not in her immediate issues instead asking "Why isn't she on methadone?" Advocating on her behalf, I eventually gained a medical response to her intense headaches, nausea, inability to eat and dizziness. I wondered how she would have fared in her first attempt to seek medical support if I had not been there. He referred her to Hospital.

For the first time in my history of working with J, she waited patiently, not swearing at anyone, curled up on a triage waiting room seat with her head in her hands, groaning softly. As we were moved through the Emergency Department, we joined the trolleys of people lined in the corridors waiting for beds, doctors or some form of medical attention. Ambulances arrived bringing others to join the sick, injured and fragile.

I caressed J's head, reassuring her; aware of her insecurity around medical staff. Her poor arms were stabbed and jabbed as the medical staff faced the challenge of finding working veins in order to obtain blood for testing. Next came a Cat Scan of her brain which revealed several tumours and resulted in her immediate admission to Hospital.

Two months later J died.

I am left with fond memories of a woman I hardly knew. A woman who enjoyed clothes and gardening, who struggled with her daughter's schizophrenia, who often slept outside the community centre and lived on the streets for years, a woman who loved Fleetwood Mac, Cat Stevens and Simon & Garfunkel. RIP sweet lady.

Sheryl Wiffen
Gestalt Therapist
March 2009

Still...On My Way

by

Seán Gaffney PhD

Abstract: Another of life's coincidences shows me that not only are we entwined threads in the complex weave of life, but also that patterns emerge and connections are made and we find ourselves in them, here using both meanings of *find*. These new patterns and connections are clearly not effects of any linear causality, with a past and present. They are emerging synchronous syntheses, making perfect InnerSense to those who experience them. Here is my experience of one such event, drafted as it happened...and its connections to other such experiences in my life. This is a description of the emergence of utterly new patterns in the warp and weave of who I am...

Introduction

In two previous InnerSense articles (Gaffney 2007; 2009) I have traced major events in my life which have formed me as I experienced them, as well as the seeds they sewed that blossomed in me, and the mixed bouquet of weeds and flowers both cultivated and wild that are who I am today. The first describes my time as a novice in a

Cistercian monastery and the novice-master's steadfast decision that I should leave the enclosed life. "You are a teacher, a communicator" father Ambrose told me. "If you want to be a priest, join a preaching order". The article continues with how I became a trainer, a language teacher, and then a senior lecturer. (In fact, I have since become an Assistant Professor!).

The second article is centred on the death of my youngest son, Dara, of leukaemia at the age of fourteen and the turmoil of my life before, during, after and since that event.

These two formative experiences in my life came together unexpectedly at a workshop at a Gestalt Therapy conference in Manchester, and then in an interview with me later in the week (Harris, 2008). The topic was how I came to choose to be a Gestalt therapist. Well, a therapist is the nearest I will ever get to being a priest, and it clearly involves caring for people and communication – not to forget that I am faculty/guest faculty at about seven Gestalt institutes worldwide. And also a widely published Gestalt author – so yes, a kind of "preacher"?

And then came my introduction to therapy. My wife and I and our two sons were in family therapy, which slowly fell apart. My wife left therapy, and each of my sons was appointed a specialist youth counselor and I continued alone with the two family therapists. And here, the shock of the sudden illness and death of my youngest son. I continued in therapy for a period, and then signed up for a 3 X 4 day Gestalt therapy residential group, determined to be a better man and father than I had been. This in turn led to my being accepted on the four year Diploma course in Gestalt Psychotherapy by the Gestalt Academy of Scandinavia. I am currently a teacher at this and many other Gestalt institutes. Becoming a Gestalt practitioner seemed so clearly to be the intertwining of two dominant threads in my life: leaving the monastery and becoming a teacher - almost accidentally, though a perfect fit; and the death of my son and its impact on me.

It was indeed this interview that gave me the inspiration and courage to write so openly about my son's death and my 22 years of grieving.

Another thread explored by Belinda Harris, my interviewer, was my obvious pride and delight in being Irish, and my unabashed joy at expressing my Irishness whenever possible. This too had become entwined with the encouragement to self-expression intrinsic to good Gestalt training.

Within weeks after the conference mentioned above, I was back in Sweden where I have lived for the past 35 years, and at my country house awaiting the 22nd anniversary of Dara's death. That was when I wrote the poem kindly published by the British Gestalt Journal in the interview. Dara's 2009 anniversary came with a meditation on our lives together, his death and my long and thorough grieving. This became the final poem in *A Journey Through Mourning*, where the intended double meaning of "Through" became so apparent

Which brings me to 2010, its emerging patterns and connections, still ongoing as I end this introduction and find a suitable heading coming into my awareness for the continuation...

It All Started with a Phone-Call

"Hi, Seán. It's Josefin"

I cannot say that I was surprised by the call. "Josefin" is a former student of mine in English and Professional Communication Skills at a major Swedish business school from the 1980s who has kept in touch ever since, usually with about two phone-calls a year, more when the topic is urgent. In recent years, her focus has been her doctoral studies and all the complexities of Academic Committees and supervisors. I recollected that the previous time Josefin had called, she was well on her way to finalizing her thesis.

Now, she was in crisis. The thesis was ready, the printer was booked – and the copy-editor had fallen ill suddenly. Since English is her second language, she needed a native speaker to read through the thesis to check its readability, intelligibility and standard of academic English. Naturally, I was her choice.

And so I found myself reading an exceptionally complex interdisciplinary study which combined economics, primary health care infrastructures, social development and psychology. All in all, a very impressive achievement, which, as I write, is still going through the checks and balances of the academic examination system.

Suddenly, in the midst of statistics and charts and policy statements, I was reading about the psychological theories of Edith Stein, a central pillar in the theoretical edifice Josefin was building. "Edith Stein...Edith Stein...now where have I heard that name" I thought. "Am I confusing her with Edel Quinn, the famous Irish Legion of Mary member? Edith Stein..."

And then I made the connection: both professionally and personally I regularly find myself in the company of both religious and secular Jews – that's where I remember the name. I remembered speaking with them about the complexities of being born Jewish, killed because of it – and then being canonized as a Catholic saint in the late 1990s...so I did 'what one does' these days: I Googled her. What follows is a very condensed summary of an extraordinary life.

Edith Stein, born and raised in a practicing Jewish family in Germany. Became an atheist in her teens. Studied first psychology and then philosophy. Assistant to Edmund Husserl, the founding father of a branch of phenomenology. Refused an academic career in Germany on the grounds of her being not only a woman, but also Jewish. Influenced by her phenomenological reading of

Saint Teresa of Avila's autobiography, she converted to Catholicism and became a teacher in various Catholic schools. Entered a Carmelite convent and continued writing, now with a decidedly Catholic choice of topics – though still in her own rigorously honest voice. Was moved from a German to a Dutch convent as anti-semitic Nazi activities increased. In an action focusing on former Jews who had converted to Christianity, she was taken from the convent by local SS and sent by train to Dachau. She died in the gas-chambers of Birkenau, August 9, 1942. Beatified by the Catholic Church in 1987 and canonized a saint in 1998, by Pope John Paul II.

I avidly read further about her early work, especially with Husserl, whose influence on Gestalt therapy is both vicarious and relatively recent. Also, the subject of "empathy" has been in the air at recent Gestalt conferences – and Edith Stein's dissertation is called *On The Problem of Empathy.* I immediately wrote to the mailing list of the New York Institute of Gestalt Therapy (NYIGT), of which I am a member, and excitedly told the strange tale of my re-acquaintance with Edith Stein, her connection to Husserl, and a possible subject for a virtual Study Group. Two people immediately expressed an interest and a third has since joined. We have been reading and commenting on her work since then, and have managed to enlist the support of major Edith Stein experts in Ireland and the U.S.A who follow our exchanges and help us with clarifying comments and references. I became a member of The International Association for the Study of the Philosophy of Edith Stein (IASPES), based at the National University of Ireland, at Maynooth College, County Meath, Ireland.

And then, out of everywhere and nowhere, an epiphany. I was musing quietly to myself about the coincidence of her death in August, 1942 being the month and year of my birth...when, almost in flashing neon, the date of her death – August 9 – broke from the page I was reading and became still in front of my eyes.

My son died on August 9.

In that instant, I knew that Dara Gaffney, 1972 – 1986 and Edith Stein, 1891 – 1942 would always be celebrated together by Seán Gaffney, 1942 - ? on August 9 from now on. And I am writing this sentence on August 6, 2010. Three days to go...

A Message from Down Under – or Up Above?

I have a very good friend and Gestalt colleague in New Zealand who works with healers, including Maori elders. I have previously been at the receiving end of messages from their Healing Circle, one solicited and astonishingly accurate. My doctor is still impressed that a group of people in New Zealand, only one of whom I have met, could pinpoint the source of poison in my body and thus support his diagnosis, even if the treatment was too late.

The unsolicited message was on my mobile phone as I crossed a bridge on Nevski Prospekt, Saint Petersburg, Russian Federation – and again they very accurately put their finger on my unwillingness to see some aspects of my life more clearly.

And now, on August 1 I get a message from my New Zealand friend, from which the following are extracts, with some paraphrased remarks to connect them. The message extracts are in *italics* and my remarks in standard font:

My friend X was glancing through your book and asked me if I would pass on a message to you. I said I would.

She said she had some information for you and that she thought you had a son who had died when he was young and if he had lived he now would be a young man. I agreed that was accurate.

She saw you sitting in a big, dark wooden chair, possibly a rocking chair, and Dara was on your knee and you were reading out loud. She had just opened your book at one of the pages with poetry on it and she said that was the moment she connected with Dara.

Yes, we had a black-framed rocking chair, and Dara would certainly have sat on my lap there.

She wondered if the room he had died in had been shut off.

Yes, his mother took over his room after his death and nailed blankets over the windows and kept the door locked.

Message from Dara via X.

'I want you to stop hiding in the dark and to stop being so harsh. Someone in the family is having a baby. It is time for me (Dara) to be reborn.'

Unsure about "hiding in the dark"...I need to give this one more time.

And okay: I can be harsh, though increasingly less so...I believe. Worth looking at.

And yes, Dara's cousin in Boston is expecting a baby "mid August"...

'I am sending you messages and you are not getting them. I am sending feathers and you are not taking any notice. They mean I am around you. "I'm here Dad". They are many coloured —purple, green/gold and you know the green/gold has a special meaning and importance.'

I am still open to understanding more of this. The feathers are a mystery. The colours are less so: purple is the colour for martyrs (Edith?) and green/gold is another though less obvious Edith connection. Maynooth College is in County Meath. The Secretary of IASPES is a local man and a follower of Gaelic football – as am I. When Dublin is playing and he is responding to some comment I have made, he will often type my name in blue – the Dublin colours. I will reply by typing his 5-letter name alternately in green and gold, the Meath colours.

'When you talk and meet someone with the same name as mine — Dara — or someone who looks like me, you shift your energy and realize you do so.'

Yes. I become confused. You, my son, Dara, take pride of place completely – exactly as you had done when I first saw August 9 as the date of Edith's death. Until the instant that the date flashed itself at me, it was exclusively your´s.

'If you are ready, bring me out into the light so I can move on.'

I honestly thought that was what I was doing by publishing "A Journey Through Mourning", not only in InnerSense, but also in my collected papers, *Gestalt at Work*. So maybe this article is bringing you further out into the light, Dara...certainly more of your own voice, anyway.

1. *You have a book that we read together and you have kept it.*

2. *There is a metal toy —it is in the dark and it needs to be on display because it was part of the family and existed.*

3. *The death certificate was wrong. Something on it was wrong. I give you this piece of information so that you will know it is me, Dara, who is providing this information.'*

I am in the country house at present awaiting the two anniversaries. When I get back to Stockholm, I'll check these out.

'I don't mince words. You need to move on to allow me to move. I am not going to leave you'.

Dara, I know you are not going to leave me. My feeling is that you need me to release you from my mourning over you, to release you by getting on with my life and letting you get on with your death. Maybe that's why Edith dropped by to see me...

'This is sent to you with love and either you accept it or you don't.'
I accept it. Believe me, I accept it.

X wondered if the green/gold had to do to with Ireland, and would be interested to know what it does mean. Also what the Gaelic words for green/gold are. Dara was really emphatic that it was green/gold not gold/green. She also mentioned that she thought English was not the first language for Dara as she found it hard sometimes to understand what he said. The accent was thick.

Yes, definitely an Irish connection. Green in Gaelic is *uaine* (oo-ahn-eh and in some dialects oo-ahn-yeh) and gold is *ór* (ore with a prolonged "o"). Dara's cousin's name almost rhymes with *uaine*.
And yes. English was very much Dara's accented second language.

The metal toy; she wondered if it was the figure of a soldier.

Yes. So did I. Though now I suspect it might turn out to be a toy car.

The InnerSense of it All

When mentioning this morning by e-mail to my friend Brian that I had a possible piece for the journal, I called it "Round 3" in my wrestling match with spirituality, the first two InnerSense articles being rounds 1 and 2 respectively.

Despite the attraction of the content in Rounds 1 and 2, I like to think I won each round by a technical knock-out – the telling of the story, the writing. Somehow, this article you are reading has written and is still writing itself and me. I had no idea until early afternoon today that I had it in me. It appeared, suddenly. I welcomed it, and here you are reading it. And, of course, if you are reading it, then it has gone through a number of filters from my First Reader to the editor and maybe more…

I have absolutely no doubt but that you, dear reader, have seen patterns and connections that I have not and I welcome any comments you might have via e-mail. For my own part, allow me to reflect on the patterns and connections I see and feel and even wonder about – in every sense of the word *wonder.*

An introductory comment: I call her *Edith.* Someone who appeared so fully in my life as I approach my 68th year, and who is connected by so many threads – teaching, phenomenology which connects with Gestalt, her death/my birth same month, same year, died the same date as my youngest son, Dara, is about to share an anniversary with him... I cannot refer to her as *Stein*, and *Edith Stein* becomes stilted after a while. So Edith it is. My recently found friend, Edith. And I will honestly try to be humble, despite having a saint as my friend...and maybe mentor?

Patterns which Connect, 1:

A most obvious pattern for me is: monastery – father Ambrose – "teacher" – Josefin, my former student – Edith.

Another is: monastery – father Ambrose – "teacher" – Dara's death - Gestalt therapist and trainer and author – Edith – NYIGT Study Group.

And then: August, 1942 – Edith dies, I'm born. August 9 – Edith dies, Dara dies. August, 2010, Dara's cousin about to give birth in "mid August".

An unsolicited message from down under connects to Dara very directly, and possibly indirectly to Edith, and probably connects me, Ireland, Edith and Dara in ways which are still unclear to me.

Reflections and Conclusions

My first thought here is the amazing way in which this paper is my current version of my annual Dara poem, which I kept space for from 1987 until 2009. My 2009 poem seemed to have closed the mourning. Dara was

"where you are in me with me now
everywhere and always"

And now, here I am alone and waiting, not only now for Dara, but also for Edith...

And, Dara, in allowing Edith to share our day together, maybe I am releasing you and moving on...so maybe your wish is being granted also in these patterns and connections...

The Latest Connections...

My latest nephew was born on August 20, 2010.

Josefin phoned me at the weekend...and, following our conversation, I decided to send her the first draft of this paper – after all, it had become possible through her work. Today, I got a mail from her to say that the deadline date of the formal submission of her thesis was

August 9, 2010, the day I celebrated Dara and Edith in my life and completed the first draft of this paper.

Josefin had spent that previous week on a retreat with the Cistercian sisters, at their convent in Norway, close to the newly-founded Cistercian monastery there. I first met Josefin as a language student some thirty years ago. Our lives have been utterly different since then at one level...at another, our very separate paths have crossed, in a sense joined, and are now inextricably linked.

The Sounds of Echoes Echoing...

My Swedish ex-wife introduced me to the songs of Carl Michael Bellman (1740 – 1795) and the singing of Fred Åkerström (1937 – 1985) when we lived in England and, since coming to Sweden in 1975, I have developed my appreciation of both Bellman and Åkerström. Amongst my favourite songs is "Glimmande Nymf" (Shimmering Nymph), Bellman's astonishingly caring lullaby for one of his "ladies of the night". Åkerström's rendition beautifully combines the lyrical with the existentially powerful. I played it in September when the Swedish participants on my specialized advanced Gestalt training were working with me in my house in the country – this is where I can play this music at the volume it deserves, and where Åkerström's rumbling bass-tones can shake the foundations rather than my neighbours in my Stockholm apartment!

As usual, I was looking at the text in my vague attempts to follow Åkerström when I found myself mumbling the following couplet about a rainbow

> "som randas lugnt och skönt
> av purpur guld och grönt"
> (striped in quiet sheen
> of purple gold and green)

Even in my own translation, I note how the rhyming scheme decides the order of the colours...

And then, two nights ago (November, 2010), I was listening to this wonderful expression of two Swedish troubadours across three centuries on YouTube and went on to "Google" Fred Åkerström.

Fred Åkerström died on August 9, 1985.

Patterns which Connect, 2:

	Birth	Death
August 1942	Seán	Edith
August 9, 1942		Edith
August 9, 1985		Fred
August 9, 1986		Dara
August 9, 2010	"Josefin's" thesis	
August 20, 2010	My latest nephew	

And so – apparently out of nowhere, the emerging figures of the dynamic field of my social existence form and connect and pattern: Dara and I, an Irish father and son who lived together in Sweden are now joined by Edith, a German Jewess, Carmelite nun and Catholic saint, and Fred, a rather wild bohemian Swedish troubadour, and almost stereotypically lovable rascal. What a quartet, and brought together by "Josefin", my former teacher-student relationship with her and her thesis...not to forget a New Zealand healer...

And Cistercians, and Gestalt, and teaching...

Somehow, the concept of co-incidence just does not support my sense of deep and meaningful connection described here, involving as it does such a rich coherence of the existential, spiritual and professional themes of my life...

So yes: still, in wonder...on my journey.

References

Gaffney, S. (2007). On Finding my Way. *InnerSense – A Journal of Spirituality, Vol 1.1.* (p. 42 – 47). Wollongong NSW. Ravenwood Press.

Gaffney, S. (2008). A Journey Through Mourning. *InnerSense – A Journal of Spirituality, 2.1.* (p. 9 – 29). Wollongong NSW. Ravenwood Press.

Gaffney, S. (2009). *Gestalt at Work – Collected Papers of Seán Gaffney. Volume 1.* Anne Maclean, Ed. New Orleans LA. Gestalt Institute Press.

Harris, B. (2008). In his own Voice – An Interview with Seán Gaffney. *British Gestalt Journal, 17.1.* (p. 51 – 56). Bristol. Gestalt Publications Ltd.

The Whole of Life — a Gestalt

by

Anne Maclean

Let's spend a few minutes considering the whole of life is a gestalt, made up of endless experiences of all sizes and shapes. This writing is the flow of ideas that have arisen when I looked at the whole to start with, rather than the parts that form to make a whole. And I could play with this for hours because in a particular, rather ironical way, I have to start with the parts to reach the whole.

So, here we go. How often do we take a look at something that happened in the past and perhaps see some new aspects emerging from the experience we have come through? Do you explore to discover what is within you now about that event and is that yet whole?

There is the gestalt of being born for each and every person on this earth. As well, there is the point at which life finishes —we die — our personal gestalt complete.

So let's go back to the moment of conception, or perhaps even before that when the thought or urge forms, and the man and woman decide to have children.

What else lies here? Have you ever wondered about creation? For us, creation happens in the dark. It would also be true to say that most ideas, dreams, visions come from the dark and arise with or from the intelligence of the person or are gifted from the mystery that surrounds, created us and holds everything in place. Or if you are blessed with sensory perceptions you may perceive and speak of your 'knowing' which is different from the knowledge that is learned. The 'seed' comes or arises from within the dark in some way or another.

The length of time that the form takes to become complete shows us the contrast of things that happen spontaneously in an instant, or for a human being, over a period of time. Life and time are inseparable and you will well know, that to understand each therapeutic encounter the time and all boundaries need to be held.

Returning then to that extraordinary process of being born, there are at least four gestalts that occur. One, the preparing for the journey as, generally speaking, the head comes down and the limbs tuck into place, then two, the traversing of the passageway as the mother's body expands and contracts and the baby moves through the birth passage. Then three, the head presents and birth occurs. Notice too, that the body tidies up as it were, as the afterbirth is expelled thus completing the birthing process.

The process of a piece of work for the gestaltist may well have these same stages. While I have wondered about this, here for the first time, I am putting words down to see what might be clearer. From time to time I've wonder if my own birth pattern has impact on how I work on any task, and particularly when I am a client, a therapist, a supervisor or a trainer. Is there any connection back to those first gestalts of birth?

Is this a useful or a useless question? At the very least as I consider how I create and possibilities arise from my senses and my mind, wondering about the energy of birth and the physical impetus of doing something for the first time holds my attention. No, I cannot be categorical but I do have a remembered sense of excitement right now as I wonder. What I do know is that sense of excitement and something new is very clear and contains considerable interest and energy. This is worth more exploration in due course.

When I take an experience I have had, because I've aged a little (or a lot) I can use my senses to deepen what I know about this, and see what emerges. I can think about it, ask for dreams to give me information, talk to someone and see what arises, or 'simply notice' whatever is present in and around me.

As I work I notice the shifts within me, and within the client. The energy of the body, of the mind and the alive essence, or élan vital or spirit provides a clear pathway that may be spoken, or simply noticed and followed. Wherever the energetic focus emerges clearly in some way or another that is where the work will start to emerge. Words will not always serve at that moment. However, a gesture, a change of posture, moving around, a sound that fits, a resting back, waiting to see, while trusting that what is central and needed has room to become crystal clear.

My workroom opens directly on to a circular lawn and the surrounding garden and one morning, some years ago now, as I stood at the doorway I had the strong feeling that I was in eternity. Just recently I came across the writings of Victor Gollancz and he wrote in his book *A Year of Grace* of the 'The Eternal Now'. As simply as day follows night, we are all part of the Eternal Now. This is where we live and have our being. In the Eternal Now there is the steady and sweet possibility of connection with the ancestors and with those who are incarnating and preparing for life. So death, life and birth abide in the Eternal Now.

So having started with the beginning of life, to finish appropriately, here is something about the end of our life on this earth.

As I have grieved for my husband Michael who died earlier this year, I explored dying and death more closely than ever before. It wasn't just the idea of dying or passing over, or the veils between the worlds. I found there is a fineness to the separation between past, now and future. Both past and yet to come are separated by a fine membrane described or experienced as a veil or a caul. So to join the ancestors the lung sac membranes no longer fill with air, and to be born, the caul or membrane breaks so the air is breathed. The two most extraordinary gestalten or events we ever experience.

In ending this writing I wondered about death and then the question, were there any similarities with being born? The word passageway comes to mind first. Birth has a passage way, life and how we grow and learn is a passage of passing days and years and the growing towards the day when life finishes. Interesting that so many people are afraid of death and yet we have come through our first passageway, the experience of birth. So in some way or another we know something about death.

Yes, death could be called a passage way or a pathway through. Our departing can be of such a vast variety I'll invite you to put your words around whatever arises as you read this. Gestalten after gestalten, and we complete this journey with our last breathe. After which others attend to finishing our time here with ashes scattered or our body buried.

Our life's gestalt complete.

Gollancz V. (1950) *A New Year of Grace.* Victor Gollancz Ltd. Britian.

Climbing Through the Scaffolding of Beliefs ~ A Reflection

by

Kerry Shipman

At the most basic human experience, we need beliefs to give us direction and meaning in our day-to-day, moment-to- moment experience of being alive. Beliefs are our reference points—our scaffolding; they assist us to navigate through complex and unpredictable events encountered in life. Some beliefs are born out of nurturing and supportive families and some are born out of traumas and disappointments. Psychotherapy as a profession is blessed (some may say plagued) by a multitude of beliefs, and the way we do therapy is based on the beliefs born out of our lived experience of what it is to be human.

Beliefs and Shame

Shame is the experience of being over-exposed and unsupported. "It is the affect of indignity, of defeat, of transgression, of inferiority, and of alienation" (Wheeler & Lee 2003:45), and our responses to these experiences are referred to as creative adjustments. The point of the creative adjustment is to ensure our survival by learning to navigate through what appeared to be an overwhelming and hostile environment. A creative adjustment for a male client who has been sexually abused as a child could be to find ways of not drawing attention to himself, to become more background than foreground, to become intensely self-supportive because seeking support from the environment holds the real potential for further abuse and injury. From this experience, a belief system emerges: beliefs such as: I must learn to stand on my own two feet, don't show vulnerability in the presence of others, and learn to solve my own problems alone. Here we have a definition, a belief in fact, of what it means to be masculine—in the Australian context at least. "[M]en are shamed for displaying too little autonomy, [and] too much connection" (Wheeler & Lee 2003:73). Some beliefs are supported by the cultural and social field. If we take masculinity in the Australian context, pragmatism wins out over idealism, individualism over community, competition over collaboration, self-containment over vulnerability. The thing is, we don't get many self-contained, pragmatic, competition, individualistic men making appointments for psychotherapy, mainly because the culture they swim in is full of affirmation of their masculine qualities and they don't need our support. Men anywhere else on the spectrum do tend to seek us out; and psychotherapy, in a real sense, is subversive in the face of the dominant discourse in our culture and society. In Gestalt, we take time to honour the creative adjustment because it got him here—he survived and did his best to protect himself—and now the original creative adjustment is getting in the way of his need to become more fully alive. Their time with us involves a process from a belief system based on 'either/or' to 'both/and'. It is a journey into relationship and connection. We can be both self-contained and vulnerable at the same time.

Whose Belief Is It Anyway?

From a Gestalt perspective, beliefs emerge through every layer or dimension of a person's experienced field phenomena. Our exposure to external field dimensions such as family, society, culture, education, religion, economics, sexuality, etc. constitute the ground from which all our beliefs manifest themselves in the here and now. Seeking psychotherapy presents an opportunity for clients to sort out the beliefs and values they have uncritically swallowed (introjects) from their past field of experiences, thus giving them an opportunity to decide which beliefs they need to keep, adjust or reject. In Gestalt, introjects are the beliefs and values we swallowed at some stage in our lives without having the opportunity to 'chew them over'. Part of my work as a psychotherapist involves working with sex offenders after release from prison and finishing off their parole. My job is to support them to reintegrate back into community after having paid their debt to society. If we portray belief as a polarity from rigid to fluid, what I find with these clients is that they are either one or the other, rarely somewhere between. From the fluid end are those brought up in an atmosphere of indifference and at the rigid end are those from a more brutish upbringing. With these clients, my primary focus is on developing the relationship in the therapeutic process.

It doesn't matter at which end of the belief polarity they are, they display an entrenched belief that they do not deserve to be seen, heard or received while displaying a deep yearning for all three. They are trapped at an impasse. From a very early stage in their development, their need for love and support was as strong as their need to avoid seeking the same. This is not an experience born out of their offending behaviour; this experience was embedded in their own childhoods. Most of these men have never experienced a mutually respectful relationship, and once they have established some sense of their own ground within the therapeutic relationship, they can reconstruct and reconfigure their belief systems in ways both grounding and relational that are uniquely theirs. They can learn to be both the river and the rock. When encountering the fixed and immobilised, they can be the river and flow around both with grace. When they need to take a principled stand in the face of coercion, they need to be the rock and trust the environment will reorganise itself around them.

It is a dance, and the trick is to know when to be which. Not all shoulds/introjects are negative of course, we should clean our teeth, and we should take care of our bodies; we should at least attempt to be respectful towards ourselves and others, and we should conduct ourselves professionally and ethically. From a Gestalt perspective, all beliefs are relevant. What is is. Once we have given a client the opportunity to differentiate which beliefs are toxic and which ones are nurturing, which are theirs and not theirs, they will have a greater ability to formulate beliefs from their own ground rather than the ground of others. How many times have we heard clients self-reference in statements like "I shouldn't feel this way", "I should be able to cope better", or when referring to others make statements such as "People shouldn't be allowed to...". My response to a client's shoulds is to invite them to reflect a little and see whether any particular person from their past pops up behind their 'should'. It doesn't take long for someone to emerge. Once this is done, I work dialogically and invite them to be that person and have a dialogue with them in the context of here and now.

Personal Reflection

Sometimes it's a good exercise to remind ourselves of our own journeys through confusion, disillusionment, and self-doubt, remembering the people who sat with us, as relational fellow beings rather than impartial observers and, in so doing, allowed us to experience what it's really like to be seen, heard and received in our brokenness and life-giving potential at the same time. When I entered adolescence, I was emerging out of an asthmatic childhood. We had left a dairy farm, relocating to a large regional town. I ended up in a class with twice the number of students as in my entire old school. Right at this point, the doctor changed my asthma medication; it was the new wonder drug called cortisone. From being a lean little kid, I became within a few months a fat blimp of a boy and the recipient of adolescent nastiness. There was a miscommunication between my old school and my new school, and I was placed in a class higher than the one I had come from. I was literally dumbfounded and had no idea what they were teaching me. The rows in the class were arranged with smart ones in the front and then according to diminishing gradations of perceived intelligence, the dumb ones were down the back. Two intellectually disabled brothers who travelled in from a farm each day were seated in the back row; my desk was just in front of them. I liked these boys because they were authentic and non-judgemental.

As I write this, I can still experience in my body my sense of overwhelm and shame—I was dumb, and everyone knew it. Not only was I dumb, I was a dumb fat blimp, and I needed to be invisible. I was pretty much at the fluid end of the belief spectrum. At the same time, my eldest sister developed a serious heart condition, so my parents were understandably distracted. In the face of such overwhelm, I creatively adjusted and learned to be very much background, because being foreground was way too dangerous. The price of course was profound loneliness. Although we were not Catholic, my parents decided to send me to a Catholic school run by the Good Samaritan nuns, who graciously made an exception and accepted an unchurched Protestant boy. The teasing continued, and I found a good hiding place to go to during lunch time. It was a giant eucalyptus tree next to the fence with a concave trunk, and I could slip into this hollow and blot out the entire school yard while observing the streetscape. What was different was that one old nun took particular interest in me and, for the first time in this phase of my life, I felt seen—not heard and received just yet, but at least seen—and it was a life-giving experience.

The nuns never put any pressure on me to become religious, and they allowed me to sit in on their rituals. I remember clearly one day when they took me to sit in on Benediction, and to this day I remember that experience as my first encounter with beauty. Suddenly I didn't feel so fluid in my beliefs anymore. When I was eighteen, I became a Catholic, not because I had faith but because I needed to belong. Like most converts to anything, I uncritically swallowed every mad belief they threw at me. As I got older, I was encouraged to be more critical and discriminating, and when I was forty, I entered a seminary for mature age men to study for the Catholic priesthood—again, not because I felt especially called by God but more out of curiosity and the deep sense of belonging. The years in the seminary were extremely turbulent for me, not because they were trying to ram dogma and doctrines down my throat but because they challenged every belief I ever had. I got my degree, but I didn't proceed to priesthood. In 2008, I went to an international Gestalt conference in Manchester, England, and attended a workshop on the history of Gestalt. Four walls had a strip of butcher's paper across them. The first person on this history line was Emmanuel Kant, then Soren Kierkegaard, Edmund Husserl, Martin Heidegger, Martin Buber, Jean-Paul Sartre, and Maurice Merleau-Ponty followed by all contributors up to the present. My deep sense of belonging was evoked and, again, not because I uncritically swallowed every aspect of Gestalt theory; to the contrary, like the seminary, my four years of training yet again challenged deeply held beliefs. One of the aspects I do love about Gestalt is its deep philosophical grounding and affirmation of the human condition. We were then invited to put on the history timeline our names and the year each of us started our training as Gestalt Therapists. I put my name down under 1980—the year I entered the seminary.

Conclusion

The reason I'm sharing this brief personal history is to remind myself that, for most mortals, we start somewhere on the spectrum between rigid and fluid beliefs. It takes courage to journey to the between and hold that space where our beliefs can be rigid and fluid, certain and mysterious, at the same time. From here we can pass from our places of shallow certainties to a place of genuine 'not knowing' and paradox. We can discover that wisdom is not to be found in what we know; rather, wisdom finds its home in our awareness of what we don't know. This is the life-space where we come home to ourselves, and from this place meet our clients. Beliefs are like scaffolding. They hold us while we explore and find our ground. They are the container that holds the ever evolving self. Scaffolding is both rigid and fragile at the same time, and we allow the container to become the content at our peril.

References
Wheeler, G and Lee, GR (Eds) 2003, *The Voice of Shame: Silence and Connection in Psychotherapy*, Cambridge, MA: Gestalt Press

Sitting Still in ElderSpirit Community

by

Anne Leibig

In 2011 I moved 35 miles from a small farm to Abingdon, Virginia, USA, a town of 8000 people in the Appalachian Mountains. I moved to become a member of ElderSpirit Community. I previously described the creation of this community in my essay "ElderSpirit Community: A community of Mutual Support and Late Life Spirituality" in Community Psychotherapy and Life Focus, edited by Brian O'Neill, 2009.

In closing my chapter I wrote:

> *In these reflections I have told part of my story, commented on risks of community building and presented tools to balance the risks as I experienced them through the lens of Gestalt Therapy. I come to Gestalt Therapy from a Masters in Social Work with emphasis on community development. My history as a community hungry person has been tempered by Gestalt Therapy and for a time I resisted the "We" of community to strengthen my "I".*

Erv Polster, a gifted psychologist has traced from Freud the contribution that has grown into psychotherapy. He explores the elements that may keep therapist from creating community and some ways of employing therapeutic vehicles to create community. He does encourage expanding "one to one" to community. (Polster,2006 p. 234) I have "expanded from "one to one" to community. Now, I am creating my spiritual path. The community has stated its mission as: *To be a participatory community of mutual support in which all spiritual paths are respected and encouraged.*

At 71 years old I am taking time for spiritual practices. One of my spiritual practices is reading and one is sitting still on the sun porch. Recently in reading about Teresa of Avila and Martin Buber I have found two quotes that encourage me.

> *"Contemplation is passive. It is a state of grace that descends when the practitioner of prayer has carved out a space inside herself through the intentional cultivation of stillness."*

> (Teresa of Avila, 2007,
> *The Book of My Life*, p.XXVII)

"It can, however, also come about, if I have both will and grace, that in considering the tree I become bound up in relation to it."

(I and Thou, Buber, 1958, p. 23)

Sun Porch Musing

Sunday

Sitting on the sun porch,
In my prayer chair, cross-legged.
I see leaves falling.
I have a good view
Of the parting of the leaves,
From the walnut trees.
The same each day,
Changing with the parting of the leaves.
I see the world out there,
Still, gray.
I am in here.
I sit still,
Having will and hoping for grace.

Friday

Looking the distance,
Blue Gray Mountain
Darker near hill,
Faded green field,
My yard,
Leaf covered now.
Inside
I see
The wilted violet
Needing my watering.

Saturday

Sitting cross legged,
The gray sky greets me,
And the bare branched trees.
I greet the sky, the trees,
The distant mountain, the near window reflection,
On the sun porch.

Anne Leibig,
270 Lowland Street,
Abingdon VA 24210 USA

My Experience of Touching Death

by

Jase C. Hodson

(previously as Gary)

Having my Grandmother, who was also my default caregiver during my childhood, die when I was twenty and then my wife (at the time) and I loosing five of our eight pregnancies meant that for me grief became central in my life. I experienced grief as catastrophic each time I faced another death or loss. It took me a long while, with many lessons learnt, with much personal growth and maturing completed before I could deal with my own loses. Yet in the end this journey with grief set me on a road of wanting to help others deal successfully with their grief, so that they may become better people in the process of grieving successfully.

Through my life since then I have been one of those men who have been fortunate enough, often through more very difficult circumstances, to have been in a number of very significant professional positions. These positions have enabled me to touch other people, often profoundly and of course by implication I too have been deeply changed.

In part due to my own losses and my subsequent personal growth in my late twenties I became a Youth Worker. In my early thirties I worked on a HACC (Home And Community Care) program caring for the elderly and the disabled. Then I had a 2 year stint at being a house husband caring for three young children and all of their needs, sadness and joys. It was around this time that I had a learning that has influenced my way of life ever since. I encountered the notions of living authentically, of allowing oneself to be vulnerable: be that I mean opening myself to God and to other people. For me this involved trying to live my life in a manner that was aware of and caring about my encounters with other people. It became about trying to ensure that each encounter was real and valuable, for both people. In my own, occasionally bumbling way, I've tried to live this throughout the rest of my life.

After learning this I was amazed to discover that I could now talk to all sorts of people at a different, deeper level, yet in a way that was comfortable and often healing for them.

These experiences were followed by another profound life change: in my mid to late thirties I became a full time theological student (training for the Anglican Priesthood). As a part of my training I becoming a part-time Hospital Chaplain and a little later, while changed role to become a part-time Parish Pastoral Assistant. The reality of these roles was that they involved me in being with people in the critical situation of their lives, often when facing their own, or a loved one's death. I had to quickly try to learn how to minister to crisis, and how to care in the face of loss, death and disaster, as well as ministering when I was fortunate enough to share with people as they encountered some absolutely wonderful joys along the way.

After three years of training I went on to be a Parish Priest, which for me soon after incorporated being an Industrial Chaplain & later an Ambulance Chaplain. In my first year in Parish I assisted in or conducted some 140 funerals & I then seriously attempted to follow up the bereaved in many of these cases. In doing so I was touched by life, by death in its many guises and by the varied impacts of loss, as never before.

Quite some years later, after coming out as gay and while struggling to retain at least some vestiges of my faith, I re-trained and became a Counsellor with post graduate qualifications in Loss & Grief Counselling. With that background I was working in a Private Hospital as a Counsellor & also established a small private practise. Over the following years in Hospitals & Aged Care Facilities I worked almost continually with people facing and experiencing death from old age, from accidents or in sudden and unexpected situation, in oncology & palliation wards and in maternity emergencies.

Towards the end of my career I was fortunate enough to lecture in a University on Counselling: particularly on 'Loss & Grief' Counselling. This actually forced me into a very worthwhile time of further research and of major reflection on my own life of personal and professional experiences. Just as significant were my reflections on the learning that other people had brought to me, learning that others had shared with me and knowledge that at times others had demanded of me.

Throughout my Pastoral and Counselling work I have continued to strive to be authentic and vulnerable. I have also incorporated a basic principal of an 'action and reflection model'. For me this has meant that I weighed and reflected on how I had worked with specific people, in specific cases. I was curious about what I had said, how I had responded to them and importantly what I thought about them - in my inner self, and what I said to or shared (sometimes about my own experiences), with these people. I was interested in why I had said something and in why I behaved as I had, as much as I was interested in what affect my words or actions had the other.

From a loss and grief perspective this model gave me valuable insights into what was effective and helpful with people facing loss and what was sometimes unhelpful or even off putting for the grieving.

More recently I have been on a Disability Pension in an unexpectedly early retirement; this is not a situation that will lead to my untimely death, but rather it's about managing continually severe pain, coupled with significant and increasing physical disability.

Very recently I had another 'fit'; the next morning I found it especially painful and difficult to move, to stand or to walk. Over the next days, and then weeks, my pain heightened incredibly and my disability seemed to affect more of my body and more of the things I wanted to do day by day. However pain was the consuming factor: I felt that I couldn't cope with it any longer, it was terrible. I am very fortunate in having a G.P. who is genuinely caring and who will actively intervene when I ask. I also have a Pain Management Specialist who is an excellent doctor and likewise a caring man as well. So if I was going to have this experience of radically increased pain and disability my professional care, coupled with having a partner who is very practical, gentle and caring meant I did have good care on hand when I really needed it.

The Pain Specialist confirmed the medication changes my G.P. had initiated: he also increasing my neuropathic pain control, then he increased it again a few days later. A week later, with pain & disability still feeling out of control my morphine based pain medication was again increased. At that point I still felt I was in pain and was aware that my leg dragged, that the pain down the other leg was awful and that my left arm was in spasm. It all seemed improved but it was still awful: I had a really hard time.

Some time later the Pain Specialist put me into Day Surgery and a few days later, after two specific procedures, I started to feel vaguely more human again. Some improvements have thankfully continued and my medications have decreased.

It is more after the event than in it, that I realise I had experienced life in a different way to anything I've experienced before. While I was on such a high level of pain medication my world narrowed down and then narrowed down again and again. Suddenly all that remained in my conscious world was sleeping like the dead, waking, occasionally wanting food or drink, then repeatedly catching myself dropping off to sleep (to the point where I dropped glasses and couldn't read a book or watch a film). Just these few functions, along with taking my medication and maybe checking email or struggling with my other health issues became the totality of my life.

What amazes me most and has become increasingly significant is that it didn't concern me in the least that that was now my life. God didn't figure, friends no longer really mattered: I recall having a vague concerns about what my partner was doing. We went shopping a few

271

times, but faced with pain, disability and sheer exhaustion I spent most of our shopping excursions slumped in the car, deeply immersed in the arms of sleep.

Since then and because of my of aiming to be vulnerable and authentic I later looked at this experience considering what it meant: what impact it had on me, my significant other(s) and my relationship to my God: was I being vulnerable in suffering? And also what did it mean to be authentic? In feeling I couldn't cope and by giving in to needing more help was I being authentic? From the other perspective of my professional commitment to an action & reflection model I needed to establish the implications of this experience to my life and more particularly the implications of this experience for the caring professions and/or religious ministry, both as I have known them and as I may be able to influence them in present carers and other professional still to come.

In the light of these two ways of weighing my recent medical experience and the psychological events accompanying it I now wonder if the implications might not actually be quite profound.

In light of my recent experience and my history of working with the dying, especially in Aged Care Facilities or in Oncology and Palliation Wards, changes in the style of care giving may need to be implemented. I recall that I used to want to pursue issues, fears and anxieties in patients about their life and death with them. In doing so I'd want to think with the patient about their own view of their salvation or condemnation, about their fears of eternal judgement. It seemed important to me to explore with patients their view of heaven and hell in terms of there being an afterlife for them; along with other possibilities such as reincarnation or a simple none existence. Additionally in a non-religious caring professional role I would specifically looked for opportunities to explore with the patient their family situations and their concerns about their family members, particularly about their spouses / life partners living without them.

Retrospectively I know that I never forced these issues on others and in fact these conversions were often welcomed, but I also whole heartedly acknowledge that I wanted to explore these issues: possibly more to make me feel better in my role than actually for the patient's benefit. Although I did this exploring as I genuinely thought that at this point in life, these issues must be critical for a patient. At times I had some absolutely profound and incredibly moving conversations with people. However I do now wonder if these conversations were only possible with people who were in a more aware state of mind than those in the state I have described myself as having been in recently.

I have now experienced a state of existence where conscious awareness of eternal issues was absolutely irrelevant. I now know it is possible not to care two hoots about life and death, about salvation or condemnation, about heaven or hell or non-existence. I also know that a previously hypersensitive person such as myself can be in a state where the wellbeing of others, even significant others, becomes basically a non-issue.

If medication or psychological withdrawal from the world around the dying person, or the seriously ill patient, dulls awareness and concerns to this extent: then the implications for the caring professions and for people in ministry are serious. What do the caring professionals have to offer people in this state? <u>Note</u>: this is not talking about <u>all</u> patients or <u>all</u> dying people; rather it concerns just those whose awareness is seriously changed, whose involvement in the thinking world is now apparently on a different level to ours.

In light of my previous work and my recent experience it would seem that people in such a state may most appreciate our pastoral/caring presence, more than anything else. Interestingly many of us have acknowledged and indeed taught the value of that presence to the unconscious person, but as far as I am aware we have not recognised its value in the situation I am currently attempting to address. 'Presence' is what I might term as the 'being there' of the carer. If someone can 'be there' in a manner that implies that no response is required, other than allowing or appreciating the presence of another person, that may be caring, and also ministry, at a most profound of levels to he person whose mind has moved out of the busy world and into themselves. My understanding of the Mercy Nuns is that they hold that no-one should die alone: therefore if a dying person had no family, friends or supporters present with them a Mercy Nun will sit with that person through all the hours of their death, no matter how long that may be. In this case – to the Mercy Nuns way of thinking, it would seem that presence was what mattered.

My conclusion is that for the dying or for those who are at a remove from the functions of people in the busy world caring and ministry must be different. What that caring may look like at its best might be 'being there' and 'presence'. That's what I would have appreciated in my recent experience and I wasn't too lost from this busy world, nor was I lost for too long; unlike many of those who sometimes spend long periods of time being seriously ill or dying in hospitals and caring institution - yesterday, today and tomorrow.

I believe that good caring and good ministry should be fashioned to meet the deeper, true needs of those who are being cared for: how best do we care for those who are either heavily drugged or those who are simply moving away from the things that consume most of us, most of the time?

This essay has been a journey into that question.